SOMETHING
WORTH DOING

SOMETHING WORTH DOING

THE SUB-ARCTIC VOYAGE OF *AQUA STAR*

JUDITH WRIGHT CHOPRA

W.W. NORTON & COMPANY

NEW YORK   LONDON

The text of this book is composed in Garamond 3 with the display set in
Centaur. Composition by The Sarabande Press. Manufacturing by South China
Printing. Book design by The Sarabande Press.

ISBN 0-393-03446-1

W. W. Norton & Company, Inc., 500 Fifth Avenue, New York, N.Y. 10110
W. W. Norton & Company Ltd., 10 Coptic Street, London WC1A 1PU

1 2 3 4 5 6 7 8 9 0

CONTENTS

❦

AUTHOR'S NOTE

The four adventurers who undertook to sail *Aqua Star* into the sub-Arctic in 1985 trusted me with their personal journals from the voyage. Without those records, this book could only have been a passage observed by a stranger from a very distant shore. My thanks go to each of them, with the hope that they will find their trust was well placed.

A special thanks to Carolann Sike, who I believe is far more courageous than she knows. Carolann trusted me further than anyone: "Write *whatever* you want to write," she said. With her permission, I have told the story from all of the vantage points available to me.

I have been fortunate in my editors at W. W. Norton, whose patience in dealing with a writer most used to finishing under 3,000 words has been much appreciated.

I would like to dedicate this book to my mother and father, who are the most dedicated people I know. Like Leslie Sike's personal god, I was interested, so I never tired of my subject. But whenever I doubted myself, my father would be sure to nudge me onward. "Is it finished yet, Judy?" he'd ask. "Yes, thank you, Dad. It's finished."

Judith Wright Chopra
August 1994

In memory of the late Carl Vilas,
historian of the Cruising Club of America,
"Don't stand at his grave and cry. He's
not there—he did not die."
—Leslie and Carolann Sike

INTRODUCTION

The world of boats—and particularly yachts—has more maver-icks than followers. Dreamers of every description follow the beats of a thousand assorted drummers down to the sea every year. They buy boats, restore boats, race boats, and look for singular things to do in boats. The yachting press publishes lists of sailing records for voyages in every direction, crossing every ocean, with every configu-ration of sails, crew, and hull. Boats the size of bathtubs set out to conquer the Atlantic and Pacific, their skippers knotted snugly into their hulls. Giant trimarans wait for winds that will push them to faster and faster crossings of the Atlantic. Every four years, hundreds of people sign up to race across the Atlantic singlehanded. A few race around the world alone. And at the other extreme, one very gentle man I know uses his 20-foot centerboard cruiser to find private anchorages other boats can't enter—his quest is for solitude with only an inch or two of water beneath the hull.

But of all the mavericks in the sailing world, those who build their own boats leave the crowd farthest behind.

The solitary boatbuilder is a person who can't buy the vessel of his dreams. Not because he doesn't have the money—chances are his dreamboat will cost him more than any production-line boat by the time it's finished. He can't buy it because no one is building it, or because no one is building it the way he wants it, or because he is driven by the need to accomplish the enormous feat of creating a living, breathing vessel from scratch. He begins by sailing other boats or perhaps just by reading about them. He progresses to dreaming about sailing to some Utopia aboard the boat of his dreams. But when he tries to identify that boat, his ego gets tangled up in it and he decides that only he can build his special boat.

The solitary boatbuilder is the captain of his own ship, the architect of his own dreams, and probably a legend in his own mind. But he's not waiting idly for his future to arrive—he's building it in the backyard.

Leslie Sike spent four years building his boat, *Aqua Star*. Every part of the 41-foot cutter was researched, adapted, built, and finished by Sike himself. He had never sailed a boat bigger than a dinghy, but he had a vision of the freedom that he could find with a mobile home on the high seas, and a staggering capacity for research and learning and hard work.

While he worked day and night to finish the boat, he began to plan a grand adventure. He was not pouring his savings, sweat, and life into *Aqua Star* just to take the inside passage from Toronto to Florida. He was building an extraordinary vessel to accomplish an extraordinary passage, and by the time *Aqua Star* was launched in 1983, he was ordering charts and installing instruments for a voyage north to Canada's Hudson Bay.

In 1985, 44-year-old Leslie Sike; his wife, Carolann, 45, a secretary; Gay Currie, a Toronto furniture-store manager; and David Farr, a Hamilton teacher and filmmaker, boarded the steel boat Leslie built and sailed from Toronto to Churchill, Manitoba, on the western shore of Hudson Bay. They each had a dream about the rewards of a successful expedition, a thimbleful of experience on boats, and enormous faith in Leslie Sike. They set out for Churchill on a rainy day in May.

Every potential sponsor of the *Aqua Star* expedition had received a brochure in the late summer of 1984. The Sikes also appealed to the media, and at *Canadian Yachting* magazine I was assigned to write a short news item: "Toronto couple plans Arctic adventure." The brochure stated that Leslie and Carolann Sike would be sailing their custom-built, 41-foot, Brewer-designed steel cutter, *Aqua Star*, to Churchill, Manitoba, via the St. Lawrence Seaway, the Labrador Coast, and Hudson Strait into Hudson Bay, in the spring and summer of 1985. They called their trip "The First Canadian Sub-Arctic Sailing Expedition," and they wanted *Aqua Star* to be the first yacht to cross Hudson Bay.

The Sikes' plan was certainly unusual. Few vessels other than supply ships and Canadian Coast Guard icebreakers venture farther north than Nain on the coast of Labrador, and no one ventures that far north for the joy of cruising. It is harsh terrain with few inhabitants and large areas of frequently ice- and fog-bound coast that are uncharted because they are rarely sailed.

The small communities are mostly summer fishing outposts, and in the earlier part of this century would be abandoned in winter as their inhabitants either returned to their bases in Quebec, Newfoundland, and Europe or moved inland for the winter to their fur trap lines. Today the people of these settlements are a mixture of aboriginal Cree and Inuit, longtime Labrador residents, Newfoundlanders, seasonal workers from all over Canada, and skilled people who are on assignment for governments or organizations such as the Canadian Broadcasting Corporation (CBC) to provide services.

As far as yachts are concerned, even the Cruising Club of America's historian, the late Carl Vilas, knew of only a few examples of sailors venturing north. A group of American adventurers sailed for Cape Chidley, the northernmost point of land in Labrador, to watch an eclipse of the sun in 1860. Another group set out to deliver a yawl to Baffin Island in 1910 and quit at the Hudson Strait—the entrance to Hudson Bay. A few hardy Crusing Club of America sailors venture along the coast today—mostly power-sailors, though, in vessels that are stabilized by sails rather than powered by them. No sailing vessel—and certainly no yacht—had ventured beyond the Hudson Strait since the early exploration of Hudson Bay in the nineteenth century. So *Aqua Star*'s voyage would be remarkable if it was successful.

Although this was the first expedition to Hudson Bay I had heard of, it wasn't the first harebrained yachtie's scheme to come to the attention of the magazine. So, with plenty of journalistic skepticism,

I went to meet the Sikes in the marina at Toronto's Pier 4. Fantastic dreams and wild exploits to get into the record books are all too common among sailors. It was part of my job to save the magazine from the embarrassment of taking the *Aqua Star* expedition seriously if it wasn't credible.

But *Aqua Star* was not the roughly finished tub that home-built steel boats often are. Her decks shone white from bowsprit to transom in the late summer sun. Tucked up at the dock, her lifelines were the first clue to the personality of her builder. They were ⅜-inch Dacron braid. Not vinyl-sheathed wire as on most yachts, but braided line—something completely different. I took in the details briefly and introduced myself to Carolann Sike, who greeted me from *Aqua Star*'s cockpit.

Carolann stood tall and spare, just on the borderline of middle age, and was smartly dressed. I could imagine her going home to a posh lakeside condominium that afternoon—this was altogether too tidy a yacht to be lived aboard and too tidy a first mate to be living aboard. Carolann told me that she and Leslie had lived on *Aqua Star* since launching her the year before, yet *Aqua Star* was ready for a boat show; neither *Aqua Star* nor Carolann fitted my picture of the casual and necessarily careless live-aboard look.

While we waited for Leslie to return from an errand ashore, Carolann gave me a tour below decks. *Aqua Star*'s interior is all brightwork: shining, polished woodwork with fitted corners and neatly finished joinery. She's deep, too; her eight-foot draft gives her a high cabin, and the companionway ladder descends to a space surrounded by the warmth of wood and the glow of brass knobs and handles. At the foot of the companionway is a junction: to starboard is the navigation station, to port the companionway continues into the galley, and aft is the passageway to the owner's stateroom and head. A cursory look at the galley told me that the equipment was first-rate and brand new. On the bulkhead I noticed a mounted, stainless steel object and instantly wished for a more thorough knowledge of instruments. What could it be? I hesitated, and then decided to risk asking.

"You know, that looks a lot like an espresso machine," I began.

"That's right," Carolann beamed. "Leslie loves his espresso." On closer inspection, I could see that it was labeled in tiny brass letters: E-S-P-R-E-S-S-O.

Carolann was my tour guide, but it wasn't clear how much *Aqua Star* owed to her efforts. She glowed with the pride of ownership in this boat but referred all questions to Leslie. I learned gradually that what *Aqua Star* owed her was twofold: Carolann had cooperated in *Aqua Star's* building with substantial moral and financial support. All of the Sikes' savings were invested in this boat, and Carolann supported them while Leslie devoted his time to preparing *Aqua Star* for sea. Just as important, she followed Leslie's lead with enthusiasm and threw her organizing skills into gathering sponsors and publicity. There was no mistaking Carolann's commitment to making Leslie's plan work. Here was a true believer. Even before he arrived on the scene, I had met strong evidence of Leslie's character in his wife and his boat.

Moving forward, *Aqua Star's* main cabin opens up into a living area with a settee and dining table and a diesel Antarctic heater. This is the heart of the boat, the place where her crew meets and where the tone of life aboard is set. *Aqua Star's* cabin is a snug place, removed from the elements outside her portlights. *Aqua Star* is designed for two people to live in comfort, with some privacy and luxury.

Leslie Sike came below just as my introduction to the boat was complete. A little under six feet tall and somewhere between burly and teddy-bearish in build, he didn't seem commanding or even particularly forceful. He spoke softly with a faded, lilting Hungarian accent and chuckled that he had only sailed dinghies on Calgary's Glenmore Reservoir until *Aqua Star* was launched. But Leslie had lived and breathed the dream of *Aqua Star* for 10 years, and here she was, straining at her lines in the September afternoon. Now he was about to start living the dream of leaving his mark on Canada by sailing the first yacht to enter Hudson Bay.

Over soup and Hungarian sausage, he told me about the building of *Aqua Star* and his quest for a quest—his search for a voyage that he could be the first to make.

Sike had chosen Hudson Bay as one place yachts had yet to explore.

From his reading and research, he felt he had found a journey that would involve a significant degree of hardship and risk. His eyes glistened and his voice caught when he described his vision of *Aqua Star* arriving in the small harbors of the Labrador Coast.

There was something of the "great white explorer" in Sike's vision. He was ingenuous and sincere in his desire to do something for Canada. Perhaps in his imagination he saw himself wading ashore with maple-leaf flags to claim Inuit villages for Canada. In the urban smugness of the 1980s, Sike seemed an anachronism, born too late to make the history books with a great patriotic adventure. At the same time, many of those who watched his preparations may have felt a tinge of envy. He was leaving the beaten path as few of those around him were capable of doing.

Sike was setting himself a challenge carefully measured for its degree of difficulty. Against the perils of harsh climate, fog, ice, and uncharted waters, he planned to pit his vessel and himself. But this was not to be a sprintlike ocean crossing: His plan called for *Aqua Star* to put into ports all along her route for provisioning, maintenance, and recreation. Unlike sailing vessels in the international Grand Prix circuit, *Aqua Star* would use her engine and all of the electronic navigational equipment Carolann could secure for them to promote. It was not the purist's idea of a man-and-vessel-against-the-ocean voyage. But it was both testing and do-able.

As Pat Healy, coach of the Canadian sailing team, commented after meeting the Sikes, "They're crazy—but what an adventure!"

Sike had built a lovely boat, but he had only one crew member and no experience with sailing. Any sailor will tell you that you can't learn the sport from books, and no amount of research or study could make the *Aqua Star* expedition a success without the sailing skills. Sailing, like driving a car, frequently calls on a person to act instantly and correctly, or risk peril. Leslie's years of reading and correspondence courses in navigation could not have given him the kind of intuitive knowledge of water, weather, and vessel that makes a true sailor. Yet, as I left with my story late that afternoon, I was strangely convinced. In the months ahead, knowledgeable sailors told me that the Sikes were crazy. When others asked why anyone would want to sail to Churchill and implied that the dream, the lofty plans for "The First

Canadian Sub-Arctic Sailing Expedition," put the Sikes on the out-
skirts of the lunatic fringe, I had no answer, but I expected to see *Aqua
Star* in Churchill. I based my belief on the evidence of *Aqua Star* herself, Leslie Sike's first boat, and on the evidence of Carolann, who supported Leslie's plans with absolute faith.

SOMETHING
WORTH DOING

"I have my own God," says Leslie Sike, *"and he looks after me because I entertain him. He's going to let me stay alive a long time. He's interested."*

Chapter One

✦

Passagemaker

In Hungary, during World War II, Leslie Sike's home was bombed. His father was a soldier, and he and his brother spent their early years with their mother, often close to danger. As a small child, he played in the rubble of bomb sites and learned a little Russian from soldiers. He says that's where he learned to depend on himself. That's where he learned to play with hand grenades and live ammunition alone but never to trust them to another child.

In 1956, when the Hungarian uprising was crushed by the Soviets, he crossed a mine field to escape from his homeland. Like hundreds of other Hungarian refugees, he was making his way to Canada via Rotterdam. He and a traveling companion booked passage on a liner called the *Waterman,* bound for Halifax. Leslie was 16, his friend was 15; they both had left everything they knew and were headed for North America with all the cigarettes they could carry. Cigarettes from all the countries they passed through were their currency: A few packs in the right places got them everything they needed as they crossed Europe.

They were teenagers on a lark, exploring the ship, making friends with its crew. When their departure was delayed from morning until 10 P.M., they bartered some cigarettes for wine and celebrated until they fell asleep. The next morning, still hung over, they missed the lifeboat drill.

As a first maritime experience, it was a disaster. On the fourth night out of Rotterdam, the ship collided with the Italian tanker *Merit* and had its port-side hull ripped open. "The steel just rolled up," Leslie recalled, "and we had felt so safe thinking nothing could happen on so big a ship."

The boys awoke to the sound of sirens and screaming in a dozen different languages. People were rushing around, racing to find life jackets. One man who pushed past them had blood on his face. They went to find life jackets too, feeling guilty and about-to-be-caught, since they had missed the drill and didn't know where to find them. They decided to tell any official who questioned them that they had been so scared they forgot where the jackets were.

In the end they found no jackets, but on deck, amid the screaming, jostling throng of passengers, they discovered why jackets were in short supply.

"People were dressed up like 250-pound canaries—life jackets on every limb, carrying suitcases and all their belongings," Leslie remembered.

Within an hour, the panic was over. The ship was not going to sink after all. In the meantime, they could see the lights of other ships twinkling in the dark sea all around them, standing by to help. They sailed under escort to Brest, France, where they were met by a crush of press and even a marching band.

After that taste of ocean adventure, Leslie and his companion decided they would forgo the ocean crossing after all, and they jumped ship with their cigarettes. They spent the evening at a nightclub, and the next day they decided to join the French Foreign Legion.

The cigarettes worked their magic, and they soon arrived at the Foreign Legion office, where they spoke fractured German to the officer who met them. After a while, he sent for a Hungarian interpreter, a stern-faced man who took them into a small room where he told them in Hungarian to go back to their ship and behave themselves.

"You go to America," he told them. "Make something of yourselves in the land of opportunity. The Foreign Legion is no place for you."

The man frightened the boys enough to send them running back to the harbor—just in time for a second departure aboard another vessel. The captain of their former ship bade a sad farewell to his 1,200 passengers, and they were once again bound for Halifax. The East Indian crew serenaded the vessel as it pulled away into open water and said good-bye to Europe.

Chapter Two

❦

Boat Builder

In Canada, Leslie prospered. He worked in the West, doing all kinds of jobs in the oil patch, footloose and ready for travel and adventure at a moment's notice. As a young teenager, he had dreamed of seeing New Orleans. And so he made it one of his early goals, soon realized.

He married three times before he was 27. "People have to take me as I am," he says. "I'm on my fourth wife now because I wouldn't change. They thought things would change when we were married, but I'd say, if you don't like it, just peel off. I don't want doilies and washing machines and hampers."

He met Carolann Aldis when he was 27 and separated from his third wife. He told Carolann a story.

"Do you know how they catch monkeys? They take a coconut, drill a hole in it and chain it to a tree. Then they put a peanut inside the hole.

"The monkey comes along, reaches inside the hole, and grabs the peanut. With the peanut in his fist, he can't take his hand out of the coconut, so he's caught.

"Do you see a pattern here? In this country, the coconut is filled with chesterfields, end tables, and doilies."

Carolann understood that if she wanted to be with him, she would have to do what he wanted to do; she would have to be ready to go—anywhere—at a moment's notice.

Leslie was appealing. "He was handsome, a wonderful dancer, a gentleman, and a lonely little boy," she remembers. "I was living with my mother, perhaps still quite naive and innocent in some ways, although I was 28 and had been married once. I had only known Leslie for three weeks. I was making plans to go out West with a girl-friend. Leslie didn't like the idea, although I didn't understand why. He told me I shouldn't go, and then said, quietly, 'How would you like to live with me?' I was so surprised I changed the subject. But the next day I asked him what he had said. 'When?' he asked. 'You know very well when,' I told him, and that was that.

"My mother disowned me because he was a married man—and a Hungarian! She 'owns' me now, but it took a long time. She still finds it difficult to accept our way of life."

They stayed in Toronto for a year, and Carolann took it upon her-self to see a lawyer to arrange for Leslie's divorce. When it was final, Leslie and Carolann were married and they began their married life as they planned to go on: doing everything together, planning an adven-ture, and putting everything they had into it.

The first adventure was a motorcycle tour of Europe. Then came a tour of North Africa. Then they switched to traveling by Land Rover and again crossed North Africa. Next they decided to leave civiliza-tion behind and build a farm in the mountains of British Columbia. While that 'sixties-style adventure was in the planning stages, they took sailing lessons on the Glenmore Reservoir in Calgary and soon abandoned their reading about organic farming and windmill gener-ators in favor of sailing magazines.

Carolann says, "We're like a couple of big kids." They choose an adventure and then put their hearts and souls into making it come true.

Leslie realized early on that you don't make a lot of money working for other people. He joked that he was thinking of becoming a street vendor with a popcorn and taffy-apple cart because they always seemed happy at their work. Carolann told him that whatever he would be happy doing was fine with her, as long as he brought money home. She recognized right at the start that Leslie was determined to be his own boss.

Then came a series of moneymaking projects, each designed to supply the capital needed for one of the Sikes' "expeditions."

Leslie's first enterprise was a massage parlor. It was at the time he and Carolann were planning their tour of Europe. They cut out entertaining and stayed home to save money. Then Leslie came up with the idea of the massage parlor. Parlors were just catching on in the West, so Leslie researched the plan, built the parlor himself, and fitted it out with tables he built. He required that applicants for the jobs demonstrate their massage technique on him— "It really was a massage parlor," says Carolann, "not one of those other places."

After five months, Leslie had made no profits at all. He took a short trip south of the border to find out how to run a profitable massage parlor and learned about advertising to attract business. Four months later, he sold the operation for triple his investment. With the money burning holes in their pockets, he and Carolann went off to explore Europe by motorbike.

To finance their Land Rover tour a couple of years later, Leslie and Carolann bought a house in Calgary, renovated it, and sold it for double the purchase price.

But the biggest project of all was yet to come.

In Spain they met a man who wanted to trade a sailboat in drydock for their motorcycle.

"That thing looks ugly and stupid," said Leslie, gazing at the ungainly object with its keel suspended above the sand. "No deal."

Leslie later found out that the boat was stolen. But it planted the seed of interest in getting to places accessible only by boat. And the idea grew stronger and stronger.

One spring, Leslie and Carolann took a drive out to Glenmore Reservoir so Leslie could practice his photography—he was particularly interested in capturing the colorful sails of Windsurfers and dinghies in the sunlight. On shore, they saw a crowd lined up outside a small building. When they asked what was happening, they learned that the people were registering for dinghy sailing lessons. At $35 each, they had nothing to lose, so they began their sailing careers in the late spring on the choppy waters of Calgary's drinking supply.

"We were soaking wet and frozen," Leslie remembers, "because we were dressed in what we thought was 'yachtie' stuff. But it was just the beginning."

It was 1975 when Leslie and Carolann began to think about seeing the world from the deck of a boat. They hung photos of the places they wanted to see all over their house to remind them and to help them concentrate on their goals. Leslie's first step was to quit smoking to finance his sailing-magazine habit. It was only the thin end of the wedge in an undertaking that would eat money and time and energy.

One day, when Leslie's magazine habit was well advanced, he heard two legendary Albertans interviewed on television. Miles and Beryl Smeeton were passagemakers and adventurers who had sailed for 20 years across most of the world's oceans. They are in the sailing record books as the first and only couple to circumnavigate west to east. The stories of their adventures aboard the yacht *T'zu Hang* were part of yachting lore that almost every cruising sailor had read and respected. Leslie was no exception, and it was with reverence that he sought out the Smeetons and asked permission to visit them.

Armed with a stack of magazines and questions about how to outfit their dream yacht, Leslie and Carolann made a pilgrimage to the Smeetons' home on their wildlife reserve in Cochran, Alberta. As Leslie and Carolann arrived in their Land Rover with British licence plates, Miles Smeeton smiled and said, "I used to own one just like it." It was a promising start to their meeting, but their different approaches to life soon took the warmth off the occasion.

Leslie was very disappointed. Couldn't Miles Smeeton tell him what kind of boat to buy?

"No. You ask me about *T'zu Hang*. I know every inch of her and how she'll behave in any weather. About the other 100,000 boats in the world, I know nothing at all."

Could Miles Smeeton recommend electronics for ocean journeys? This question infuriated Smeeton.

"*That's* our electronics," said Smeeton, pointing to a small, battered transistor radio, "and it has been for 25 years."

Leslie was aghast. Smeeton had rounded Cape Horn three times—although he had twice been dismasted. Leslie believed Smeeton had to have all the answers. Maybe he's just tight with money and advice, Leslie thought.

"But what if you get into trouble?" Leslie asked.

"If you're going with the idea of shouting for help, you'd better stay here!" Smeeton answered vehemently.

That lesson was the first and most memorable of many he learned in the next five years—it was five years before Leslie knew what kind of boat he wanted, then ten years of research and planning and saving to the day of *Aqua Star's* launch.

Meanwhile, there was money to be earned and Leslie was in search of a challenge. He was doing a lot of work in the construction field and began to find fault with the "little boxes" that builders were putting together for a seemingly never ending parade of buyers drawn by Calgary's booming oil economy.

"Have you ever noticed that they put all the plugs in the same places—as though everybody has the same lamps and everybody arranges the same furniture the same way?" Leslie asks.

He and Carolann put all of their money into financing an ideal home. With ideas borrowed from home shows and magazines and model homes, Leslie built a house that was subsequently photographed for the front page of a Calgary magazine. Just before the Calgary real estate market took its legendary dive in 1980, the first people to see Leslie's dream home bought it. Now Leslie and Carolann had the money to go from a dream home to a dream boat, and Leslie had finally read enough and learned enough to make some decisions about what that boat would be like.

First and foremost, it would not be a production-line boat—like the dream house, it would have to be custom built to Leslie's precise specifications. He decided to build it himself.

Every choice relating to this boat was made with elaborate research and investigation. The process was so thorough that Leslie became an expert on the workings of marine equipment and electronics. Already a skilled construction worker, he became a skilled boatbuilder for the boatbuilding project.

To choose the optimal size for their boat, Leslie and Carolann went through the "Passage Notes" columns in five years' worth of *Cruising World* magazines, adding up the lengths of the ocean cruisers featured in each issue. Their average length was 39.5 feet. Leslie decided that his boat would be 40 feet.

Somewhere along the line, the boat was given the name *Aqua Star.* Like every other decision relating to this special boat, it was thoroughly researched and proven to be one-of-a-kind in the often-copycat field of boat names.

Leslie researched the relative properties of wood, fiberglass, aluminum, ferrocement, and steel as boatbuilding materials. Only steel, he concluded, would survive a collision with a whale or an iceberg. He decided to accept the chore of painting the steel hull in return for the safety of its strength. "Steel is the strongest and most forgiving material," says Leslie. "Steel will give you a second chance."

Then there was the choice of designer. Ted Brewer's steel full-keel cruisers were known for their ocean voyages, and Leslie easily narrowed his choice to Brewer's 41-foot (not including its bowsprit) cutter for seakindly performance.

A thousand other decisions were made as plans for the building of *Aqua Star* progressed. Everything that went into *Aqua Star* was selected with Smeeton's warning in mind: "If you're going with the idea of shouting for help, you'd better stay here."

Nonmagnetic Ormiston stainless steel wire was ordered from England for *Aqua Star*'s rigging. And every piece of equipment was checked for true marine conditions—nothing that was only token "marine grade" went into *Aqua Star.* A year before the brightwork went on the deck, Leslie mounted a piece of teak on the cab of his truck and coated it with samples of the varnishes and oils available. The varnish that lasted and protected best was the one that went on *Aqua Star.*

The choice of building yard for *Aqua Star*'s hull was relatively sim-

Lead for Aqua Star's *keel came from hospitals and service stations, collected piece by piece and then melted and poured into 40-pound ingots.*

ple: Many Brewer hulls have come out of Huromic Metal Industries' yard in Goderich, Ontario, on Lake Huron. Leslie decided on a special hot metal zinc spray (galvanizing) to protect his hull, and he determined to have it built "his way." In order to be on hand while *Aqua Star's* hull and deck were built, he decided to live in Goderich. Carolann made plans to live with her mother in Toronto, earning money to support the tremendous appetite the unborn *Aqua Star* was developing.

With many important choices made, Leslie and Carolann next began to collect lead for *Aqua Star's* keel. Carolann would dress up to go out and buy lead from gas stations, counting on distracting the station owners in order to buy the metal cheaply. Later they read about a boatbuilder buying lead from hospital X-ray departments, and they arranged to do the same. In the basement of their home in Calgary, they melted lead and poured it into 40-pound ingots. When they had 8,400 pounds, they rented a truck to transport it from Calgary to Goderich. The building of *Aqua Star* had begun.

CHAPTER THREE

❦

ARCTIC MARINER

Leslie poured the lead for *Aqua Star*'s keel himself. "The guys at Huromic were metalworkers, not boatwrights," he explains. "I knew just where I wanted the lead." He lived in the town of Goderich on Lake Huron for two years, until *Aqua Star*'s hull was almost complete and could be put in the water. He worked day and night, sleeping on board, dreaming of what he would do with this special boat.

Alone in Goderich, Leslie began to think of a destination for *Aqua Star.* He was still reading every piece of marine literature he could get his hands on, studying navigation by correspondence courses, and planning a grand voyage that would make the record books. He began to reflect on his life.

"By the time I was 16, I'd lived through a world war and a revolution," he explains. "Canada gave me a home, and I wanted to find a way to give something back."

A Canadian "expedition," sailed "by Canadians for Canadians" was what he wanted. This boat was not just a cruiser—she was built for northern waters. With the same thorough, even elaborate, research, Leslie decided that Canada's far north would be *Aqua Star*'s destination. Leslie Sike had never sailed anything bigger than a dinghy on any body of water bigger than the Glenmore Reservoir, but he was determined to take *Aqua Star* north.

Leslie moved *Aqua Star* from Goderich to Port Credit in June of 1981. In Port Credit marina, he built a frame tent around the boat and lived first under the cradle steps and later on board. In the marina, he found himself among friends. "I could talk to sailors and no one would know I hadn't had 20 years of experience." He was in good company there, with a group of other independent types building their own boats, and he joined with them to form the Boatbuilders' Co-op to buy parts and materials. He made friends with the man working next to him in the yard, and one day he told his neighbor that the rigging wire connections he was installing looked inadequate.

"Metal and glue together don't make sense in a marine environment. You should sit down and look at it and it should make sense," Leslie told the man. Leslie went with an all-stainless system; His neighbor stayed with metal and plastic. A few years later, Leslie received a letter from his friend, who had been dismasted when a wire joint gave way under stress in a 25-knot wind.

In May of 1983, *Aqua Star* was ready to be launched. Here was more proof of his ability to accomplish wonderful things alone. The rest of the world just didn't measure up.

"I wanted the lake to be cleaned for my beautiful boat," Leslie recalls.

"He was Mr. Hyde," says Carolann. "Whenever he had a great deal of pressure on him, Leslie could be horrible. *Aqua Star*'s launch brought out the best and the worst—it was so important to him that everything be perfect, that every detail should be thought out. It was his biggest dream becoming reality."

Leslie and Carolann moved aboard *Aqua Star* in Port Credit, and gingerly they began to learn to sail this dream boat, always planning and preparing her for an important voyage.

While Leslie continued to finish *Aqua Star*'s interior, Carolann worked for Air Canada in downtown Toronto. Their sailing was limited to short trips on Lake Ontario that could be accomplished by two

At Aqua Star's *launch in Port Credit, Leslie Sike's boat was perfect—Lake Ontario was found wanting. Leslie and Carolann lived aboard while completing* Aqua Star's *interior and fittings.*

people, and they continued to research an epic northern voyage that, in Leslie's words, "would set us apart from the other five billion people on the planet."

Leslie came up with the idea of sailing into Hudson Bay, and soon he and Carolann had read everything available about the Labrador Coast and Hudson Bay. They scoured libraries and bookshops, learning about sailing in northern waters and crossing their fingers, hoping not to find any record of a yacht sailing into Hudson Bay.

Sailing in the north brought images of cutting through ice—and of Henry Hudson's abandoned vessel trapped in Hudson Bay in 1611. During the summer months, the ice that moves down from the North Atlantic disperses, but large bergs and pack ice—large fields of ice that can crush a trapped vessel—can still be found. Not seen but very dangerous to small vessels are "growlers"—large, tumbling bergs that are hard to spot at night and can severely damage a yacht's hull. The danger of ice is real, but in summer, fog and heavy weather are the most significant threats to shipping along the Labrador Coast and have frequently been responsible for marine disasters. And, of course, although following a coastline sounds safer than sailing in open ocean, in fact the lee shore is the great danger for ships of all sizes. All in all, it seemed that the voyage to Hudson Bay would be sufficiently dangerous and demanding to "set them apart."

The Sikes gradually defined their voyage as "The First Canadian Sub-Arctic Sailing Expedition." They set a departure date of mid-May 1985, based on the ice season, and went about organizing the gear they would need to complete the journey.

Radar and a dinghy were high on the list of missing items. They would need crew and a photographer. But asking others for help of any kind, even as sponsors or crew members, was not something that appealed to Leslie.

Finding crew was the most important task, however, since both Leslie and Carolann recognized that without at least one other person, they could not count on completing the journey before the ice returned to Hudson Bay in October. It was going to be difficult to find experienced crew who were willing to undertake a five-month expedition in unknown territory with an untried captain. And, too,

Leslie and Carolann posed with Aqua Star *for their publicity brochure.*

perhaps the time had not yet come when Leslie was willing to share the glory of the expedition.

If asked about whether they had found crew, Leslie would shrug and say, "We'll go without crew if we have to."

In midsummer of 1984, the Sikes printed a color brochure describing their expedition for potential sponsors. They also sent it to the yachting press and local newspapers, resulting in a harvest of interested well-wishers, plus a few small human-interest articles in the Toronto papers and the yachting media. It marked the beginning of a public relations career for Carolann, who spearheaded the task of finding sponsors to provide missing gear and placed *Aqua Star*'s sub-Arctic expedition squarely in the public eye.

CHAPTER FOUR

✳

CAPTAIN AND CREW

In September 1984, Leslie went shopping for a chair he could modify to fit at the chart table aboard *Aqua Star*. In a shop on Front Street in Toronto, he explained his requirements.

"A chair for a boat? You should talk to Gay," the clerk told him, calling over a young woman working nearby. "Gay is a sailor."

Gay had been listening when she heard Leslie say that he wanted the chair for his yacht. Now she approached, smiling broadly and full of questions about *Aqua Star*. Leslie soon discovered that the store didn't have the chair he wanted but he invited Gay to visit *Aqua Star* and come sailing aboard her.

Leslie told Gay about his plans and his boat. He told her about his wife—his good buddy who had contributed so much to the creation of the boat.

That was Gay Currie's introduction to "the expedition." She came aboard for one sail and then another, and before long she had given notice to her boss at the store so she could work full time raising money and finding sponsors for the expedition. Gay was a gypsy who had caught the sailing bug. She was also ambitious, and she was drawn to the expedition as a way of adding to her sailing credentials. She too wanted to make her mark.

Always a tomboy and good at sports, Gay went to a private Anglican girls' school and on to university in a co-op study program at the University of Waterloo. Her parents, she says, spoiled their children with experiences. They traveled constantly during holidays and school breaks and gave Gay a taste for staying on the move. The co-op program allowed her to alternate her English studies with work terms where she would gain practical experience in the writing field. It seemed like a good plan for a woman who liked nothing better than a change of scene.

Since leaving university, Gay had traveled to New Zealand, San Francisco, and Florida, where she and a friend had signed on as crew to sail to the Azores. After that, she had spent 15 months as a stewardess for Royal Jordanian Airlines, finally escaping the tight control and sequestering specified by her contract to land back in Toronto, where she worked at a furniture store while deciding what to do next.

Gay Currie joined Carolann Sike in an all-out effort to find sponsorship for The First Canadian Sub-Arctic Sailing Expedition. During the winter of 1984 and early spring of 1985, the two spent many evenings putting together proposals for potential sponsors. Little by little, they found 53 companies and individuals who would donate cash or gear to their project. Alex Tilley, the flamboyant Canadian (not, in this case, an oxymoron!) haberdasher to adventurers and sportsmen, gave them Tilley Endurable clothing; G. B. Pennel gave them warmly lined white foulweather gear; Vuarnet gave them sunglasses; Kodak gave them 35mm film; the charterboat *Southern Star,* now moored near *Aqua Star* at Queen's Quay, gave them an evening cruise to give away as a door prize at a fund-raising party; and the list went on and on.

Meanwhile, the expedition was still without a photographer. One of the precepts of the voyage was that the crew of *Aqua Star* should document what they found as she traveled up the St. Lawrence, along the Labrador Coast, and through Hudson Strait into Hudson Bay. It was an extension of Leslie's fascination with getting to places that could only be reached by boat. Part of his gift to Canada would be a record of what he found along the way. But spring arrived, and still no one had applied for the fourth berth aboard *Aqua Star.*

Finally, a Hamilton cinematographer and teacher, David Farr, read about *Aqua Star* in *Canadian Yachting* magazine and called me there to inquire about the expedition's need for a photographer. In short order, he committed himself to being the fourth member of her crew, and to supplying the cameras and gear needed for both still photographs and 16mm films of the voyage.

Farr claimed no knowledge of sailing, however. His boating experience was limited to a little houseboating on the lakes, but he was ready to learn. There was only one real drawback: Farr was a teacher and could spare no time to work with the crew and get to know them and the boat before the departure date. He remained a man of some mystery to the others—one more item in a surprise package they would open on May 18, 1985.

Carolann and Gay were becoming expert at getting the media on their side. With press releases and telephone calls, they secured a healthy degree of attention for the *Aqua Star* expedition throughout the spring of 1985. Matt Phillips, a cameraman with Toronto's CITY TV, was often seen "on location" filming *Aqua Star* and her crew during promotional events. Phillips had accompanied a CITY reporter on a reconnaissance visit to *Aqua Star,* where he met Gay Currie. Phillips soon became a regular feature, spending as much time with Gay as they could both spare from their chosen careers. Phoning Matt, waiting for Matt, and meeting Matt became the bywords of Gay Currie's days—so much so that Leslie and Carolann occasionally doubted her commitment to the expedition.

It was the first source of conflict in a friendship that had run smoothly from the start. Unlike Leslie and Carolann, Gay had not spent 10 years planning this expedition, and whenever Gay's desire to see Matt overcame her desire to work on *Aqua Star,* little seeds of doubt were planted and nurtured. While Gay was 27 and in love, Leslie and Carolann were 45 and weighed down with the responsibilities of their crusade.

In talking with each of them during this period, I found it clear that Leslie and Carolann had set the boundaries of their lives very precisely. Everything that was important to them was aboard *Aqua Star* and every activity of their days was related to pushing the expedition closer to reality. When they spoke of the future, it was of arriving in Churchill, Manitoba, after the crossing of Hudson Bay. Their future extended only as far as the winter of 1985–86.

Gay, on the other hand, saw the expedition as a springboard into her future. She spoke often of what was to come after the expedition. She played with ideas of writing about the expedition, buying her own boat and sailing away—a whole range of plans that completion of the expedition would make possible. Now that she had met Matt, everything that was important to Gay would come at the end of the voyage.

While sponsors seemed to be supporting the expedition more and more, there were others who voiced serious doubts. One man, a sailor from the Royal Canadian Yacht Club, warned Leslie and Carolann that their plan had no hope of succeeding. From the great height of his experience of sailing the Great Lakes, he looked down upon their homemade expedition to Hudson Bay and declared, "If you go, you won't come back." And he was not alone.

The climax of the fund-raising activities was a huge party planned and organized by Carolann and Gay at Toronto's Harbourfront. All of their sponsors, family and friends, and the press were invited to the lakeshore complex that is a focus for boating and tourism in the city. Harbourfront provided the room; Harbourfront's Queen's Quay restaurants (which had come to know *Aqua Star* while she was moored at the quay) donated the food. There were door prizes and displays and speeches and a noisy crowd of well-wishers who were getting on the bandwagon just as it was ready to leave. There were also curious onlookers—people who wanted to know what these newcomers to the sport were up to and what made them think they could pull it off.

There was one surprise that evening. One of those who had read an article about *Aqua Star* in *Canadian Yachting* magazine was Bill Nicholls of Calgary, frontier support coordinator for Canterra Energy

Ltd., an oil exploration company. Canterra was going to drill pilot holes for oil in Hudson Bay that summer, so Nicholls had contacted Leslie Sike to offer Canterra's support in the area, should they need it. Sensing that the long-hoped-for radar and dinghy might be at hand, Leslie Sike decided to approach Nicholls with his wish list of still-needed gear. "We are still looking for a major sponsor," he added. At the *Aqua Star* party a week later, Canterra Energy Ltd. announced that it would supply all the missing equipment and act as the expedition's major sponsor. With that single stroke of good fortune, the expedition acquired the cachet and credibility it had lacked. The simple fact that Canterra was putting its resources behind the project gave the crew and their supporters convincing evidence that Leslie and Carolann and Gay and David had a chance of arriving safely in Churchill, Manitoba. The blue-blazer crowd bit their collective lips and resolved to wait and see.

At *Canadian Yachting,* the voyage had gathered enough momentum to attract the attention of my editor-in-chief, who was invited to dinner with Leslie, Carolann, and Gay aboard *Aqua Star.* The next day, she called me into her office.

She was concerned that I might have endangered the magazine's credibility by becoming associated with the *Aqua Star* expedition. Her dinner aboard the boat had led her to believe that Carolann and Gay were completely dominated by Leslie Sike. And none of them had the experience or skill required to succeed. Since I had already written about *Aqua Star* in the magazine, the damage was done, but she felt now that we should step back.

In retrospect, I think some of her reaction came from the fact that the inquiry into the sinking of the *Marques* and the lawsuits that followed were still making headlines. The *Marques* was a square-rigged wooden ship sailing from Bermuda to Quebec for the "Quebec 1534–1984" gathering of tall ships when she was overturned by a sudden, violent storm. Eighteen passengers and crew went down with her, including Ian Brims, a longtime associate of *Canadian Yachting* who had been commissioned to write about the trip for the magazine. After the shock, sadness, and horror came a circus of legal actions and media reports—some responsible, some purely mean-spirited—that found fault with tall ships and even sail training itself. The U.S. lawsuits against the owners of the *Marques* claimed negligence; the American Sail Training Association was under fire for allowing young people to become involved in an activity as hazardous as sailing square-riggers. It wasn't surprising that at the time my boss felt the magazine wanted nothing to do with an expedition that didn't have blue-chip credentials.

But I also think she had seen something I had missed. I wondered if Leslie's good humor had slipped on the evening of her visit. When I was with them, I saw only three new friends who had found a singleness of purpose. While I recognized that Leslie was holding all of the reins, I saw only a rather insecure captain. I couldn't help contrasting Leslie with another Canadian sailor I know.

A well-known ocean racer and delivery skipper, he gave my husband one of his first sailing lessons, casually offering him the tiller of a small yacht on a windy fall day. When the wind gusted, my friend, sitting on the rail with his sweater in the lake, smiled, refused to take the helm back, and calmly instructed my husband to swing it over and right the boat. I contrast that sail with one a few weeks later aboard *Aqua Star* with Leslie Sike. No one took the helm—under motor or sail, in the channel or on the open lake—except Leslie Sike. I thought he made the transit of Toronto's Western Gap—just a short channel between Toronto Island and the mainland—into something akin to rounding the Horn. I figured that because he had built the boat, he simply couldn't let anyone else have the pleasure—and, after all, he was still gaining confidence in his own ability. As Gay once noted, not only was Leslie a "nervous Nellie," he was "a Hungarian nervous Nellie to boot."

At the magazine, the editor-in-chief finally resolved to wait and see. Like many others, she felt that since Canterra had become involved, the expedition had gained credibility. At the very least, Canterra's communications support on Hudson Bay would be a tremendous asset. I was going to wait too, but I still felt sure that I would see *Aqua Star* in Churchill.

· · ·

At the same time, more than the pessimism of yacht club and other assorted naysayers was worrying Leslie Sike. While Gay and Carolann and David built their faith in the expedition on Leslie's confident demeanor, Leslie himself was lying awake at night with thoughts of the Strait of Belle Isle and every other threat to his boat that lay between Toronto and Churchill.

The St. Lawrence itself was judged by local sailors to be a formidable hazard. Even experienced sailors exclaimed, "The locks! The locks and the currents make it an obstacle course." Working day and night to prepare *Aqua Star* for the voyage, Leslie had ample time to consider the task he had set for himself and his crew. At every step of their way, a new challenge would lie ahead of them: the locks of the upper St. Lawrence, the currents of the lower St. Lawrence, the shipping channels, stray ice, fog and currents in the Strait of Belle Isle, the pack ice of the Labrador Coast, the open waters of Ungava Bay, the unknown waters of Hudson Strait—plus whatever lay in wait for them during the crossing of Hudson Bay.

Leslie took some comfort from the fact that every piece of equipment aboard *Aqua Star,* every feature of her construction was "overbuilt," as engineers say, stronger and more secure or powerful than it strictly had to be. He knew from the beginning that his crew was the weakest link in the chain, and his answer for that weakness was to take every task, every decision onto himself. As the countdown began for May 18 and the official departure of *Aqua Star,* he had mentally shouldered the entire burden of sailing the yacht to Churchill.

Carolann, knowing Leslie well, tried to prepare Gay and David for the Leslie they would meet when they were underway. His pleasant manner and easygoing charm could disappear, she warned, when Leslie was under pressure. It was hard, though, for them to imagine that this genial and welcoming man could be less than warm and enthusiastic, and they filed away Carolann's warnings with all of the others, not to be taken too seriously.

CHAPTER FIVE

※

TORONTO TO QUEBEC CITY

May 18, 1985, was the day chosen for The First Canadian Sub-Arctic Sailing Expedition's "official" departure from Toronto. The Sikes were determined to lift this cruise out of the range of a cold-water holiday and into record books—perhaps even history books. No media contact was overlooked—in Toronto or anywhere else along their route. Like the public relations pros they were becoming, for their staged departure Carolann and Gay planned a media event with Toronto's mayor, Canterra's representatives, a bishop to bless the expedition, and the Toronto harbor fireboats to salute it as it headed for the Eastern Gap and on to its first stop in nearby Whitby.

The morning of May 18 was cold and rainy. Aboard *Aqua Star,* cognac was poured ceremoniously and the crew was tense with excitement fueled by a stream of well-wishers, family, and friends who stopped by with gifts. One of the first brought a copy of the *Toronto Star* with a photo of the crew of *Aqua Star* in full color across the first page of its "Lifestyle" section. Carolann and Gay gave one another a pat on the back for their efforts.

Later on, Leslie's brother arrived. He had just received news that their mother had died in Hungary.

Leaving Toronto behind, the crew sailed Aqua Star *to Whitby, where she was provisioned.*

"She was a rough old girl," said Leslie, quickly dismissing condolences and going on with his preparations below decks. On this day with so much to think about, there was no charity for his mother, but perhaps a little anger that her death was intruding, like the rain, on his momentous occasion.

Later, standing on the podium with the mayor, he humbly thanked the supporters of the expedition and sincerely promised that he and his crew would accomplish their goal of sailing to Churchill in spite of any hardships that might befall them.

The mayor gave the crew the best wishes of the people of Toronto. Bishop Snell, the Anglican bishop invited by Gay's mother, said a prayer for those who go down to the sea in ships. It was Drake's Prayer, taken from his words before he sailed into battle in 1587, asking God to grant the knowledge that "There must be a beginning of any great matter, but the continuing unto the end until it be thoroughly finished yields the true glory."

The crew of *Aqua Star* was so self-conscious, so tense and excited that morning, that I doubt they took in the bishop's words. But Drake's Prayer has been passed down through four centuries because

SOMETHING WORTH DOING   ✌   31

those who take up "great matters" must keep their goal always before them. Long-distance sailors—perhaps anyone who takes on a task that involves endurance—use the concept to get past "the wall," to finish the voyage when everything about it has become painful and distasteful. And the crew of *Aqua Star*, among themselves and in their diaries, often spoke of the need to focus on getting to Churchill in spite of any current degree of hardship on board.

After the prayers, Carolann and Gay gave bouquets of flowers to their nervously smiling mothers. And then the rain stopped dripping lightly and began to flow in torrents across the quay, sending everyone running for shelter inside the terminal building. I said hello to a man I recognized from the yacht club. He shook his head and nodded toward Leslie. "Bloody fool. He's got no business going up there," he said gruffly, and hurried into the crowded building.

Soon afterward, *Aqua Star*'s crew—dressed in their smart, white, donated foulweather gear—cast off her lines and Leslie turned her bow into the crowded harbor. With the charter yacht *Southern Star* following behind carrying Gay's parents and Carolann's mother, *Aqua Star* headed for the Eastern Gap, dodging the Royal Canadian Yacht Club's entire fleet, out for its annual sailpast.

They were underway, on their first sail together as a crew, with only one sour note. The cameraman shooting their departure from the deck of *Southern Star* was Matt Phillips, not David Farr. David was on *Aqua Star* watching the action, but, Carolann noted, not filming it. They left *Southern Star* behind at the Eastern Gap and turned to look east to the passage ahead.

Gay's and David's diaries give us glimpses of the real life behind the formal send-off that day and throughout the voyage. They wrote in them almost every day, unlike Carolann and Leslie, who made notes and then put them into diary format when the voyage was over. Leslie wrote with a view to publication: "A steady rain fell as lines were cast off and *Aqua Star* moved away from the dock on her historic voyage...." His after-the-fact diary even has a title—"All's Well That Ends Well." Leslie characteristically adopted the professional skipper's policy of writing in his log every hour and at the end of each day throughout the journey. That record is purely factual—details of course, weather, and mechanical information such as engine speed and temperature. No emotions muddy the captain's log, which is regarded strictly as a legal document. Carolann wrote regularly until Quebec City, but after that only sporadically, because her frequent bouts of seasickness made writing too difficult. When Carolann wrote in her diary, she was very conscious that someone might read her words, but just occasionally she wrote what she felt without censoring herself. Gay used her journal to spill off all the emotions that coursed through her mind moment to moment. Her journal tracks the melodramas and relates the highs and lows in *Aqua Star*'s crowded cabin—it's the very personal record of a volatile personality.

What David's diary lacks in extremes of emotion and colorful language, it makes up for in detail. While he was struggling with the elements to make a film of the trip, his diary tells the story clearly, with quiet asides to vent some of his own stress, which was rarely glimpsed by the rest of the crew. David began and ended the voyage as an enigma to the others. Carolann and Gay, the most forthright of women, began to think that there was something lurking behind his composure. They presumed that still waters ran deep. He seemed so quiet, so retiring and imperturbable that eventually they both presumed he was sneaky. It was a case they couldn't fathom. They knew he must have thoughts and wishes he wasn't expressing, and they speculated privately about what they could be.

With four such varied personalities on board, the ritual of writing in their journals gave *Aqua Star*'s crew an important outlet for tension in addition to a means of recording their experiences.

Gay's diary for May 18 begins confidently:

> May I write religiously every day during this voyage, and provide an enjoyable, honest account of our experiences.
>
> Bright blue skies as I'd requested. Sizzling good mood (a rare occurrence for me in the morning).
>
> Fire Department boys motor up to confirm the time of our water salute. They inform us that we have an article in the

Toronto Star. I'm barely mentioned, which does bother me because I've worked hard for this project—no pay, all heart, boat doesn't belong to me. I will complete a unique trip with increasing skill as a sailor, deeper understanding of people, enriched catalogue of memories. The least the press could do is publish my previous experience sailing and work as a promo person for the last eight months! I got the bloody story in the Star and would have appreciated the bloody publicity for myself.

Well, selfish expressions aside, the article was accurate and well-written.

12 p.m. Steady gathering of public and friends at boat. Leslie is in a good mood too. We have a quick shot of cognac and a bear hug. I'm thrilled this day has arrived and so is he. I now have good vibes re personal relationships throughout the voyage, contrary to my feeling during the past few weeks of preparation. Stress doesn't look good on any of us!

I spent the afternoon kissing, hugging, shaking hands, and smiling and felt right at home the entire time. I found Mayor Eggleton to be genuinely warm, relaxed and enthusiastic.

This expedition means a lot to me. I'm happy and peaceful and anxious to learn. I have a sneaking suspicion this will not be my last adventure. . . .

David Farr is keen to learn—a little too keen at the moment. Conditions were a little rough and I'll be more willing to teach him when we have more time and calmer conditions. Leslie agrees.

Gay was at last taking up the role she had been training for, but with an eye to the future. She focused immediately on what the expedition would mean to her later, on a résumé or a book jacket, on the boost it would provide for her next adventure.

For David, the newcomer, the day had its own complications. He was keenly aware of his ignorance about sailing and clearly valued every chance he had to learn. His first sail and his first real chance to meet the rest of the crew were public events that made him doubly uncomfortable. But the joy of beginning the great adventure had infected him, too.

Massive quantities of supplies, equipment, and spare parts had to be stored in Aqua Star's *hull. Carolann took charge.*

Last few hours seem like years . . . very anxious to get on with it. I dislike farewells, especially those that drag on, but realize that it is an important occasion, the culmination of the first stage—preparation.

I'm unable to film because of the rain. I'm encumbered by an orange Mustang foulweather suit, but warm and dry. The other three crew members are enveloped in white Pennel rain suits and white rubber boots. I feel conspicuous and wish I also had whites on.

Since this was the first time, ever, that I'd sailed, the other crew members, as well as myself, waited apprehensively to see how I'd respond to this new environment. Experience had dictated half a Gravol pill to be taken in advance, so physically, to everyone's relief, I weathered our first leg, a four-hour sail to Whitby.

I find it exhilarating, but feel so helpless, as the other crew members tend the mysterious maze of lines and cables. I pitch in, wanting to learn so I can contribute to our passage. Although I'm an encumbrance, the others patiently explain some of the skills.

The crew had an uneventful sail to Whitby, where they planned to spend two weeks provisioning *Aqua Star* and fitting her out—radar, mast steps, and a crow's nest were still to be added. A mountain of provisions was stowed in *Aqua Star's* hull, and everyone worked to finish the preparations for departure. Gay commented on Leslie's mood as they completed their projects:

Carolann is lovely and relaxed. We get along well...David Farr is quite cheerful and is supportive of Carolann and me. On the whole, I feel we've got a good team. Leslie will be back to normal once we really get going. Today he's in a foul temper.

Leslie's foul temper was directed that day at Carolann: Against Leslie's specific instructions, she had bought plastic containers for stowing provisions in *Aqua Star's* hull. Leslie's objection to plastic was that in a marine environment, and particularly in a steel hull, condensation is a constant, and that moisture would be trapped by plastic and cause mildew and other problems.

But Carolann was faced with the problem of storing five months' worth of provisions and materials. Plastic containers would allow her to keep provisions dry and, at the same time, structure the storage space. "I knew that they would do the job better than anything else, so I did it and took the response from him in my stride."

It was the first of many times that Leslie accused Carolann of being against him. With all of his responsibilities and the self-imposed pressure of total control of the expedition, he felt lonely and occasionally sorry for himself. Leslie would say that he was the only one who cared enough to be constantly on duty, on watch, and the others were just along for the ride. This was a rod he had carefully crafted for his own back by refusing to delegate. At the same time, the crew had such faith in Leslie that they rarely second-guessed him, and for the most part relaxed while Leslie did the worrying. Eventually

David came to the conclusion that Leslie made everything seem harder than it really was in order to make himself feel important—but that was months later, when shipboard life in cramped quarters had taken its toll on interpersonal relations.

David noted the tension, adding that he was glad to see that soon after tempers flared, everyone was back to normal.

When all the provisions were stowed and gear organized, they were unable to wait any longer in Whitby for equipment Canterra would supply, so they arranged for Canterra to send the gear to various ports along their route.

In the busy days between the staged and actual departures, Gay took time off to be with Matt before they were to be separated for three months. When she came back to the boat, feeling a little low and indulging herself in missing Matt already, Leslie let her know that she had allowed the expedition to come second to her personal life. Gay scrawled an angry reaction in her diary—she despised her position as unpaid crew and cook most bitterly whenever Leslie and Carolann reminded her that they owned the boat. It was a demoralizing tactic for the Sikes to use, particularly when she had worked so hard to contribute to their success, but Gay always focused on her own need to make a success of the voyage to overcome her disappointment at not being recognized.

Once again they set off in the rain. With the mayor of Whitby and enthusiastic boaters to cheer them on, the voyage of *Aqua Star* was underway.

Then, for a few weeks, there was a kind of phony expedition, a chance to settle into *Aqua Star,* to learn a little about one another while doing only the most ordinary kind of boating. They moved slowly along the north shore of Lake Ontario, stopping at the larger ports to take on equipment and provisions.

Lake Ontario sailing was familiar to the Sikes, who had cruised the lake often since launching *Aqua Star.* The ports all have facilities for "transient" boaters, as marinas call visiting yachts. In contrast with the north shore of the St. Lawrence River, the facilities on the lake are closely spaced and relatively easy to enter, and the towns are large and bustling. At the towns of Cobourg and Kingston on Lake Ontario, and all through the St. Lawrence Seaway, the crew sought dockage that was accessible to transportation and shops for provisioning, while at the same time inexpensive and secure from both weather and theft. With the expedition's limited budget, Leslie and Carolann could not afford marina dockage at the $25 and $30 a night that some places charged. David noted that whenever possible, they would anchor offshore to rest rather than pay overnight dockage.

At every stop, Carolann and Gay made sure local officials, radio stations, and newspapers were notified that the expedition had arrived. In port, the crew settled into a routine of running errands, doing chores, and entertaining visitors—from town mayors and the media to curious fellow boaters. And they continued to pick up supplies—such as the $800 worth of groceries donated by A&P Food Stores they collected in Kingston.

Ten days after *Aqua Star*'s formal departure from Toronto, she was still only in Cobourg, some 80 miles east on the north shore of the lake—usually a one- or two-day sail. Some aspects of their daily lives were already established. For example, the fact that Gay was not a morning person was abundantly clear. Since her berth was on the settee in the center of *Aqua Star*'s main cabin, she was in the way if she slept longer than anyone else. And everyone eventually realized that if she wasn't wakened, she slept on.

> Leslie woke me up at 8:50 A.M. "Woman, get up."
> Next time, I will tell him, "My name is Gay."

Everyone was sizing up David Farr. Both Gay and Carolann felt threatened by David—Gay because she was afraid her role in the crew would be taken by him, Carolann because she was alienated by Leslie when he had another man to chum around with. Even in the early stages, the crew of *Aqua Star* was often divided into "the boys" and "the girls." In the little ship's company, Gay wanted to be considered the first mate, or at least the apprentice first mate—earning her ticket, taught and trusted by Leslie. In that she was already foiled to some extent by Carolann's official standing as half-owner and captain's wife. Having David aboard made Gay constantly watchful and resentful whenever she felt in danger of being considered "just the cook." Leslie often preferred to teach him, give him responsibility. And David was

eager to learn and easy to get along with, although clearly an introvert in a crew of extroverts. Gay was always ready to defend her
territory.

> David's a strange guy. He's a bit too smooth and yet I feel
> sorry for him a little because he's trying desperately to fit in.
> He's with Leslie most of the time, which is fine with Carolann
> and me. My only concern will be if he inhibits my learning
> opportunities re navigation, etc. David is overly concerned with
> Carolann's well-being. Wish he would just relax.

As they entered the Thousand Islands, Leslie was very conscious of
his lack of experience. The charts had to be read accurately through
the scattered islands, and *Aqua Star*'s eight-foot keel required a deeper channel than most yachts. And beyond the islands loomed the hazards of the St. Lawrence Seaway.

Essentially the locks are chambers in the waterway with massive
automatic doors at each end. When the door facing your boat is open,
you enter and take your place along the walls or rafted to the next
boat, waiting without moving until the door behind you is closed.
Then the level of the water in the chamber changes—going down-
river, the chamber empties. Here the difficulty is holding your vessel
along the walls while allowing it to float lower. Finally, the door facing your vessel is opened and there is an orderly (everyone hopes) exit
from the chamber to the new level of the waterway.

The locks call for skilled boat handling in close quarters. For
sailors, this is a test of how well the yacht maneuvers under power
(often a problem for sailboats, which seldom reverse as well as power-
boats), how well the crew handles lines, and how smoothly the skipper coordinates the whole operation. On the seaway, however, locking
is complicated by the sizes of the ships involved and the size of the
locks—water-level changes sometimes are hundreds of feet. *Aqua
Star*'s 50 feet overall made her a very small fish among huge lakers—
commonly so long that their crews require bicycles to get from bow
to stern quickly. The big ships are so difficult to maneuver that it is
almost impossible for them to avoid smaller vessels—the skippers of
small vessels must be constantly on guard to avoid them. The seaway

is the sort of obstacle that can worry a skipper horribly until he has seen it and tried it.

Leslie, as everyone had already learned, vented his quite natural tension with all manner of verbal abuse, usually directed at Carolann. And Carolann accepted the role of Leslie's safety valve. He felt he could vent his anger on Carolann without causing a mutiny, and she was proud of the role she played, although both David and Gay noted that they felt Leslie treated her unfairly.

Approaching the first locks, *Aqua Star* encountered her first adventure: shad flies. The early part of the day had been idyllic. Gay's diary only hints at one of Leslie's explosions:

> Made a nice breakfast of cereal, strawberries, and cream. Sunrise very lovely. Leslie is nervous and excited—feelings which are manifested through a little ill temper and impatience, usually taken out on Carolann. Not fair.
>
> After lunch we hooked the motor on the dinghy in order to drop David and camera overboard. We then sailed around him

Shad flies were everywhere—even inside Leslie's sunglasses as he steered. That night the sleeping bags were alive with them.

for some good shots. . . . Blue herons spotted from time to time today.

At about 1 P.M., *Aqua Star* and crew headed into hell. A swarm. Brown clouds. Shad flies in a sexual frenzy flew, crawled, fluttered, clustered, mated, invaded us. Never in my life! My flesh was crawling and they got into the boat too. The aft cabin was alive. Strangely, we all stayed fairly calm, particularly Leslie and David and Carolann. Me, I just kept whacking my head from side to side to keep them out of my nostrils and mouth. We were all laughing actually (with pursed lips). David was funny. He started to count them. Carolann moved and he had to start all over.

Leslie and I murdered and tortured a few. Suddenly I realized that the crow's nest was above all this so I escaped for the remaining 20 minutes before we arrived at Iroquois Lock.

We tied up in the old canal and pulled up the sails, washed and scrubbed the deck, which was completely black with them.

Hot and brown and exhausted, we all had rum, dried apricots, and nuts and sat around talking about our behavior in such shocking conditions.

The flies stopped when night fell. Hope this isn't an indication of trials along the way.

The next day, David fell overboard while fending off—the black, slippery remains of shad flies left his deck shoes without their usual traction. He held on to *Aqua Star* desperately with one hand while Gay and Carolann tried to haul him aboard. The effort left him with a seriously sore arm throughout the next few months.

Otherwise, the locks themselves were not the hazards they had seemed. "The St. Lawrence was just like highway driving," said Gay. Only one small incident received some attention in the crew diaries. Gay noted:

From Iroquois Canal we headed into the first two locks, the American Eisenhower and Bernard Snell. Never having been through before, we were all a little bit anxious—some more than others. Leslie must learn not to take out his anxieties on his wife!

David learned today not to interfere with Carolann's boat work. I learned that I cannot throw 1/2-inch 100-foot line around a floating bollard inside the lock.

Even Carolann commented that their first attempt at coordinating locking procedures had been flawed:

> Went through the second lock today. They use floating bollards (marvelous), but had difficulty removing the aft line, because it was being handled by too many people and had been overcleated (I received lots of abuse over this). Next lock I shall handle myself—too many cooks spoil the broth.

The cruising life, apparently, was going to involve putting up with a certain amount of vitriol from Leslie Sike, but they weren't going to let it spoil the fun. David painted a picture of life on the seaway:

> We pass several locks on our way to Montreal. The weather is again gorgeous. The American locks have floating bollards which we weren't familiar with but the second time we did a splendid job in securing to them. We pass a few lakers, which is interesting and provides a diversion. We all wave to each other. I am pleasantly surprised at how well *Aqua Star* rides out the wash from those huge vessels. The countryside is very pleasant to view. We pass cities and towns yet there is very little boat traffic. From our point of view the communities look very peaceful and sleepy, with church spires adding to this illusion. We realize, of course, the hectic, frantic busy lives people are caught up in. But the life on board our ship probably looks pretty serene to them. We are all really quite busy. We must still adjust to each other and our cramped environment. Even motoring and not using sails, we are all occupied: Leslie plotting our course, one of us at the helm, and the remaining two peering ahead for channel markers. Then there are meals to prepare—Gay is the cook—and pictures to take, as well as journals to be kept up. There is not much time spent in making beds—just straight-

ening sleeping bags for Leslie and me in the aft cabin. The women sleep in the lounge, which is (a) the only other room and (b) also the living room, so they roll their bags each morning and stuff them in sacks. We keep our clothes in duffel bags, so one can imagine the shape they are in. I generally fold my pants into a mound and use them for a pillow at night. We have no hot water unless we heat it on the stove, but to conserve fuel we only use hot water for coffee and to wash the dishes. We are the unwashed. Arising in the morning around 4 A.M., we rush into longjohns and sweaters, over which we pull on our one-piece cold weather suits (they resemble snowmobile suits). We then each carry out our duties and tasks necessary to get underway. This varies with conditions such as wind, etc. The first few miles are busy ones in getting ourselves settled onto our course. So washing or shaving are almost nonexistent from day to day. Brushing our teeth is the only luxury we take the time for. I washed a pair of socks today. They now reside on the aft deck, entwined with anchor rope so as not to blow overboard.

This afternoon we went under our first lift bridge. We approach very close and the light remains red. We start to circle and when we do, the green light goes on and the bridge lifts. There is no other traffic and we wonder why he waited. The first vehicle stopped by the bridge going up is an ambulance with its lights flashing. "Two birds with one stone," Leslie says sarcastically. "We helped make his day."

Our next bridgemasters are more co-operative, and although locking through is tense, we are becoming more confident and skillful, as now we know what to expect.

Montreal marked the end of the first 500 kilometers—4,000 to go. Arriving in the marina at Port Sainte-Hélène, the crew jumped onto the dock. Leslie bear-hugged Carolann and Gay and wrung David's hand. "Well, we've made it this far."

A three-day stopover in Montreal gave the group time for sightseeing, dinners, and more public relations. They made the front page of the *Montreal Gazette,* and more equipment from Canterra caught up with them: rifles, ammunition, thermal underwear, Arctic boots, elbow-length mitts, and radar cable. The residue of the shad-fly invasion was scrubbed from *Aqua Star*'s deck.

Aqua Star left Montreal for Trois Rivières on a Saturday morning (Leslie refused to leave port on a Friday, following the time-honored superstition among sailors). With the current in the river, *Aqua Star* was given a boost of speed and could make six knots and more rather than her usual five under motor in the narrow channels. This was exhilarating speed for the crew, as David noted:

> We leave around noon for Trois Rivières, Quebec, and travel the 72 miles in eight hours. Our log shows about 50 miles, so current has given us over 20 free miles. We are delighted. I was at the helm all the way. Early in the afternoon I had to veer to avoid running down a duck with half a dozen chicks strung out behind her and one on her back. The day is overcast and very still. We pass channel marker after channel marker. It's very pleasant motoring and we are all in a good frame of mind. Leslie stays below at the charts, ticking off the numbered markers as we pass them, occasionally popping his head out of the companionway, like a groundhog.

Arriving at the industrial north-shore city of Trois Rivières, a tense moment was the catalyst for the development of some crew spirit. David praised Leslie's cool handling of the situation and remarked for the first time that he felt part of a team:

> We approach the Trois Rivières Marina cautiously. As we turn in, we are horrified to find the current sweeping us sideways toward the shore of boulders. Even as we gain headway with a burst of engine power, we fear the narrow channel (narrow for our large ship) and the apparent lack of a mooring space. But the boat owners standing on the dock recognize our plight and quickly move several boats to make room for us. We seem to be approaching rather quickly, but good control by our skipper and some skillful handling of our fore and aft lines successfully conclude a very tense mooring which left us all shaking.

We quickly retire to the marina lounge and after two beers each, richly deserved, we relax and joke and laugh. Nothing like sharing a harrowing experience to knit a crew together.

Carolann commented that she wished our skipper had reassured her that he was taking appropriate action to counteract the drift. [Carolann had screamed, "Bloody hell, do something!" a split second before Leslie raised the engine's rpms.] Gay thought of moving fenders from port to starboard, because of the boulders. I felt that I had to decide on one of two alternatives—whether to make a swan dive or a jackknife over the side.

On a layover day in Trois Rivières, the conversation over dinner turned to frogs and the different methods of using them for bait. Animal lover Gay exploded:

Carolann, David, and I go for beer. I cook a really nice stew. But after two beers and 1½ glasses of wine, I got upset and loudly verbalized my disgust when David and Leslie started talking about burning frogs. I was genuinely mad, so I stomped out. Leslie said I should just disappear quietly. I retorted that he never does. Oh, and then I got the truth, loud and clear: "It's my boat," he said. Oh, so not until I have my own boat can I burst forth with emotion. Went up to the clubhouse feeling sick and in tears. I hate and loathe and despise these scenes and yet I've fallen into them before. I get thick with people, jump in with all four feet, and then I get hurt.

Carolann came up to clear the air with me—she's good that way. She says I should use my femininity to manipulate in a positive way, be assertive and don't drink too much 'cause I get emotional. Feeling like an asshole—quite frankly. We talked for some time, but I did not want to go to the boat until 10:30 so the guys would be in bed. Don't know how to handle Leslie now. I can't be anything but myself, and he'll just have to learn a little bit too—that he's too sensitive. I will be more businesslike, just do my crew job and keep my mouth shut. . . . And I'm not going to try to please everyone either! We all cater our asses off to Leslie and he punches you in the nose for it. I like him, but I now realize that I mean nothing to him. He'd actually be happiest with autohelm, I think.

But Carolann had a different perspective:

Leslie became very upset and angry with Gay because she didn't appreciate the conversation. They were having a bit of fun and were encouraged when they saw how irritated Gay was. She was very abrupt and told everyone to change the subject. Leslie felt she should have just excused herself and left. I feel had she asked more politely, everyone would have obliged. She has been very coarse and becomes agitated with people on and off *Aqua Star,* acting like a spoilt and arrogant person. She does not like to be known as "the cook" on *Aqua Star* by the media, although she is always referred to as our crew. She had gotten her dander up more than once while dealing with the media, making them feel embarrassed and uncomfortable. Her attitude is not appropriate and I felt that I should warn her, as Leslie will not tolerate it.

Leslie himself is a very difficult person to understand and can be very trying at times, but he is the captain and it is his vessel. He is concentrating 100 percent on this venture and expects others to do the same.

There is no drinking while under sail, but once into port and all duties have been taken care of, everyone is free to enjoy themselves (as long as alcohol is within reason). We have noticed Gay's overindulgence in this area and have said nothing. This is also when she becomes rude and misunderstanding of others. I have tried to inform her of Leslie's feelings and that Leslie is not the easiest person to get along with himself, but that she must try to work around this (she knows Leslie's personality and that he is also quite charming at the appropriate time).

Relationships on board were still being established. And, in spite of his temper, Leslie was not completely vilified. While Carolann was defending Leslie's right to be obnoxious, David was appreciating

Leslie's patience in explaining even the most obvious aspects of boat handling to a novice:

> I ask Leslie a silly question: "At this marina, there is a tide. Do we tie up differently?" He patiently explains that it's a floating dock.

En route to Quebec City from Trois Rivières the next day, *Aqua Star*'s stuffing box leaked, letting large amounts of water into the bilge. Very simply, the stuffing box is a necessary hole in the hull that is sealed against leakage. Located in the stern at the point where interior steering controls are connected to exterior fittings, such as the propeller shaft and the rudder, the stuffing box is a vulnerable point in a vessel's hull because of the possibility of leaks if fittings or gaskets shift.

Leslie quickly found a loose clamp on the rubber sleeve at the propeller shaft. With the clamp tightened and a few seconds of work from the engine-driven bilge pump, everything was back to normal. Leslie logged it as "Crisis number 1."

Earlier in the day, he recorded a small but typical example of his profound self-reliance:

> Turned on the VHF for a weather report, but it's in French only. Since I don't understand it, I do my own forecasting by keeping a very close eye on the barometers. Every hour I record readings—temperature, wind direction, and a whole lot of other data—in the log. I have two barometers on *Aqua Star* because I believe in them. At 8:14 A.M., we pulled away from the docks—good-bye, Trois-Rivières.

That day, Leslie announced some changes in the crew duty roster. In her outline, Carolann gives Leslie all the credit, although Gay commented that she thought Carolann finally must have gotten through to Leslie.

> Today we changed our system somewhat. Rather than David at the helm all day (because he likes it there) and Gay preparing all the food, Leslie made a change to include everyone and

Washing dishes aboard Aqua Star *was frequently Carolann's chore. Later, icy salt water was used, and utensils became scarce when many were inadvertently thrown overboard with the dirty water.*

have them constantly involved in all aspects of sailing the ship. For instance, David prepared breakfast; Gay and I did the dishes, lowered the dinghy from the deck and tied it aft, and stowed our shore electrical cable. Leslie of course is constantly overseeing the entire boat with specific mind to navigation, engine, pumps, and of course the anchoring, docking, and coming in and out of harbors. He takes ultimate responsibility for everything that happens aboard *Aqua Star* while underway because of the constant change of direction in channel, narrowness, and the great number of container ships going and coming, and also because this is a first attempt at the seaway. We also had a one-hour-on and two-hours-off helm each while Leslie was navigating and keeping constant check on tide and current.

This was how Carolann worked—taking complaints and feedback from Leslie or Gay or David and acting as a conduit to resolve the situation. It was a case of being the meat in the sandwich, and it eventually led to impossible strain on Carolann.

CHAPTER SIX

❦

QUEBEC CITY TO
NATASHQUAN

Arriving in Quebec City for five days of waiting out bad weather, doing maintenance, and provisioning, the crew of *Aqua Star* was very conscious that they would soon be in the Strait of Belle Isle, and that what was wrong aboard the boat would get worse if it wasn't resolved. In three weeks of sailing that would seem undemanding compared with the trials of the Labrador Coast, the list of interpersonal problems had become fairly serious.

First and foremost, whatever Leslie's burdens, his verbal abuse of Carolann and occasionally Gay was making the atmosphere oppressive. Gay herself caused tension in a number of ways. As a semi-vegetarian, she was eating more of the fresh foods, which were disappearing quickly and eventually would become scarce. The position of ship's cook is also a difficult one: Hungry crews demand food on time (not a strength of Gay's) and to their taste—in this case, extremely varied. David, for example, described his favorite meal as a bowl of cereal with fruit and milk. Leslie's tastes were more adventuresome—hot peppers and spices. The best cook in the world couldn't please everyone, every day. And to make things worse, Gay frequently had to abandon her own meal. Since Leslie was first to be

Aqua Star *moored in historic Quebec City.*

served, he was first finished and would give orders to clear the cockpit or cabin and prepare to get underway before Gay had eaten.

And Carolann was in the middle of the conflicts. She put herself in
the role of loyal wife to Leslie, defending him to others, while he
berated her constantly—often over complaints about David or Gay.

I am not worried or frightened of what is ahead. I know that
we will be suffering a lot, but I am concerned that the others
can't appreciate Leslie's reactions to certain situations. He is not
an easy personality to understand. Even after 19 years, I can get
very frustrated and fed up with his ways, but then I also see and
know other aspects of his personality—charm, wit, perfection-
ism, a self-made man who has and is still accomplishing his
dreams and his visions in his own way. An example: One day
David said to me, "Leslie sure is difficult sometimes." I asked

what he meant. "Well, everything must be done Leslie's way." I replied, "Yes, because he has had to depend on himself since a very early age when the majority of people are protected in a family setting. Leslie had to look after himself and therefore depends on himself and has confidence in himself—a quality, by the way, which is lacking in a great many people and one which creates jealousy in others toward him." Yes, with Leslie as the song says, "My Way" has gotten him this far in his life and he will not be changed to suit anyone, not even me. I like that.

Gay and I do of course have our tiffs, but nothing ever amounts to much because we both hate an uneasy atmosphere and therefore are very upfront and honest with each other—which, I might add, we find the fellows unable to be, not only with us, but with each other.

As a treat in Quebec City, the crew spent an evening at a Middle Eastern restaurant, complete with cushions on the floor and a belly dancer. Leslie was apprehensive about leaving *Aqua Star* unwatched at the marina, and only with much coaxing did he agree to go along. Carolann put his reluctance down to Leslie's worries about what the future held for the expedition. Gay noted, however, that it was a good evening. Carolann was lighthearted and flirted with David, although Leslie was out of sorts. The next day, dinner was late, and Leslie stormed off in a temper. Another bad scene and more tension. Finally, Gay explained, they took the bull by the horns:

Found David in lounge at marina house, writing. He stopped when I entered and told me that he, Carolann and Leslie had had a serious discussion at lunch re Leslie's verbal abuse and foul language and that the atmosphere and relationships must clear. Carolann was in tears all day and will leave the boat and the expedition if things don't improve by the Strait of Belle Isle. I would miss her—we at least have open, healthy communications. . . .

Escaped to two glasses of wine and letter to Matt. Leslie is angry. I can tell and I cringe. We're all getting a lesson in psychology.

Tense and ugly atmosphere on board. We confront Leslie. Leslie says that he cannot afford to have feelings, nor worry about whose he tramples. He is also aware of a problem between himself and Carolann. We've yet to see what changes, if any, ensue. . . .

I was tired at 7 P.M., but Carolann talked me into going for a walk. Leslie's talk with each of us seems to have cleared the air. He seems a little more relaxed. I hope he learns that a captain must be in control, commanding respect from crew, setting a fine example and atmosphere. Till now I've felt bullied a little and totally unappreciated. He said as long as he does not shoot me, I am being appreciated, and not to take his abuse personally. Okay.

Preparations for leaving Quebec continued, and each member of the crew made the most of every chance to get away from the boat and the others. David finally broke his silence in his diary:

Gay cooks breakfast. She nearly blows herself up when she adds alcohol to already blazing burner. Then she proceeds to fry three eggs in a half-inch of bacon fat, telling me this is how Leslie likes it. But Leslie isn't here and the eggs are for me. I mention this and she coldly replies that she is not the cook. I don't understand, as she is writing a cookbook about this voyage. [For the first part of the journey, Gay wrote out recipes for some meals and detailed all of the provisions she used.]

I go shopping and walk miles, enjoying the old parts of Quebec as well as the new. . . . It's nice to be away from all the squabbling among the crew members. They are like children.

Aqua Star left Quebec City at 3 A.M., on Sunday, June 16, bound for Isle aux Coudres. As the yacht sailed downstream, the tide and current gave her many knots of free ride. The St. Lawrence here becomes so wide that they could not see its south shore. Rugged hills line the north shore, where the communities rely on the railway for supplies. Now the crew began to feel as though they were on an expedition, rather than a cruise. Since they were always traveling north and east, the days steadily grew colder, in spite of occasional spells of summer warmth. Their sleeping bags were their only real refuge from the cold while underway, and they relished them after early morning watches, going below decks tired, hungry, and cold.

At St. Bernard Marina, they found that the Quebec provincial government's pamphlet on its new facilities for boaters was overoptimistic: There were no facilities, but a little old man at the dock nevertheless charged them full price. The Quebec tourist bureau had published the pamphlet in 1984 to encourage boaters to visit during the Quebec 1534–1984 celebration. One of the celebration's highlights was the Transat–TAG yacht race from Quebec City to St. Mâlo, which was expected to attract cruising boaters to explore the lower St. Lawrence. Some of the facilities promised in the pamphlet took a few years to materialize.

Gay hoped that when Leslie and Carolann went for a walk to explore the village, they might clear the air:

> I hope they have a good talk 'cause Carolann is so unhappy. She wants to enjoy this voyage, but she's not – Leslie giving her shit when she's at the helm for not being accurate, etcetera. Oh, I hope things cheer up. I feel wonderful inside.
>
> Tried to explain a little bit about sailing to David—thought he might appreciate it. Don't think he thinks I've got a brain in my head. He asked my opinion about changing the reach of the mainsail. Then when I looked at the direction of the wind (we were wing-and-wing, in a light following wind) and checked our course to steer on the chart and as a result decided the main was fine where it was, he acted as though he didn't believe me. That's why men are aggravating. They grow up thinking that women have nothing valuable to say. Fine. I won't waste my sweet intellectual breath on dead ears. (Oh me and my little outbursts. . . .)

As it happened, Carolann went for a country walk by herself. She was rarely so unhappy that she couldn't be refreshed by the sight of a bright sky and tree-lined shore. She took photographs constantly, made tape recordings of people they met, and faithfully washed dishes and cleaned the boat in spite of her seasickness. Her joy in being on *Aqua Star* and her appetite for fun and excitement were rarely diminished. She never thought of herself as the martyr that David's and Gay's diaries sometimes made her seem.

From St. Bernard, Carolann, Leslie, and David took the ferry to Isle Sainte Hélène, where they enjoyed "lip-smacking" hamburgers— their last for a few months.

Back on board, Leslie spent time plotting his course for the next day.

I got the charts out and plotted our course to Tadoussac. The tide, according to my calculation, would be high water at 4 A.M., so we would have to leave here no later than 2 A.M. One should worry about the tide only from Trois Rivières to Tadoussac because of the relatively narrow river. After Tadoussac, the river widens so much the tide will not affect your sail-

Leslie fished here in Havre St. Pierre, Quebec, when his responsibilities gave him time to relax.

ing. I also prefer to arrive in a strange port during daylight hours, even if it means leaving the previous port at night. So I told everybody, "Sleep fast and set the alarm clock for 1 A.M."

The night was short. Seemed I just put my head down and the alarm went off. Gay made some cereal and fresh coffee and we were off. At the start there wasn't any wind, so we motored. Later the wind came up, but—you guessed it—right from the northeast, so we continued to motor. I sure am glad that *Aqua Star* can carry 200 Imperial gallons of fuel.

We saw an unusual amount of freighter traffic this evening, but these guys are good—they keep an eye on you. Sometimes you can see them altering course a long way ahead so as not to give you a heart attack. I made contact with one and I asked if they could see me on the radar since I don't carry a radar reflector. The radio operator answered, "I could see you 12 miles ago." So if you have a steel boat, at least they know you are out there somewhere.

At one point in the river the channel was very narrow. There was a big ship coming up and one going down. I wasn't sure whether there was enough room for them and *Aqua Star*, so I went outside of the channel marker and stopped until they had passed, then I continued. All of a sudden there was a big blast on the horn thanking me for my courteous, seamanlike conduct.

Only Leslie could interpret a horn blast so clearly!

Although Leslie could be a sailing purist in some respects, he was always prepared to rely on *Aqua Star*'s engine rather than lose time waiting for the wind to change. He felt that meeting a timetable for the expedition demanded an engine. If *Aqua Star* was to move out of the St. Lawrence as one season's ice receded and enter Hudson Bay before the next winter's ice arrived, he had no choice but to motor whenever conditions made it necessary. This was sometimes frustrating to Gay, who felt she would have enjoyed the challenge of a "true" sailing voyage. But realistically, the voyage without an engine would have been unlikely to succeed.

As usual, David's journal moves beyond the highlights to fill in the minutiae of the day's passage:

Up at 1 A.M. Breakfast of bran flakes. Cast off at 2:05 A.M. A freighter is passing the harbor so we just follow him. As he disappears out of sight, dawn is breaking. It is a lovely clear night with stars twinkling. The radar is great—we can follow the freighter even if we can't see him. It also shows a boat coming behind us. We circled when it got close and fell in behind it. It's cold today—longjohns and down jacket under Mustang one-piece foulweather suits. Girls are using wool ski masks. Earlier we had three-foot seas, but now only one-foot. We are on one-hour watches and Carolann spends all her time in her bunk because Leslie gives her a hard time. Gay is late twice in taking over watch from me. First time 10 minutes, and then after a few minutes on watch she excused herself to go to the head. This last time, Gay is stretched out in the cockpit, looks at her watch several times. When she is 15 minutes late, she gets up and asks if I mind if she goes to the washroom first. I mention she is late again and she gets very defensive. Carolann and I go to the head before our watches and still we are five minutes early.

We love the scenery. The water is now green instead of brown. From Quebec on, we've been following the north shore, about one mile away. Hills and valleys rugged and pretty. Those ahead are lighter shades of gray in the mist. Leslie is getting on to tide tables and spends nearly all of his time below plotting and checking our position. Occasionally he sticks his head out of the companionway and peers through binoculars at distant range markers and then pops down out of sight again. He reminds me of a groundhog. Especially with his beard.

The girls sleep in sleeping bags spread on lounge seats. Carolann is very tall and takes up ⅔ of the U-shaped couch. Gay is very short and only needs ⅓. Carolann can't abide the mummy bag and because we anticipated a fifth crew member and carry an extra bag, she zips the two together. Although the lounge sleeping isn't very roomy, they can stand easily and use the main head, which is quite roomy. They can also access the galley, a step away. Leslie and I have very tight quarters in the aft cabin. Turning over as we sleep cannot be achieved unless we are wide awake. Since we don't have heat on, early morning is quite cool. It seems the best solution for me is to spread my cotton liner like a bottom sheet and not get in it. Too difficult to get out without waking Leslie. Then I spread the open sleeping bag over top of me. Again, it's too warm inside it.

As we approach Tadoussac Marina, the tide is rolling in. It has a leading edge and along this edge the water is jumping and nervous—a strange sight.

We see our first whales, which may be orkas. Although they are all about the boat, they are some distance away and we can't get pictures. First we see them spout, then their backs appear as smooth black tubes.

We dock at beautiful Tadoussac Marina, a small cove. As we debark, a gentleman on the dock introduces himself: Harold Price. He invites us to jump into his station wagon (displacing his huge black Labrador dog, which pants and dribbles down our necks).

He drives us around town for a look, drops us at a restaurant, and drives off yelling directions to his house for a 6 P.M. cocktail out the window. After lunch the girls walk in the town. Leslie and I return to the boat for a couple of hours' sack time. Later, sitting writing my journal on deck, a heavy-set man (whom I'd observed on a motor launch nearby) comes over to visit. He talks about his 44 years on ships. He captains a ferry here. During our conversation I learn we have mutual friends in Kingston. I hope to see him tomorrow. He speaks of the beauty of the Saguenay River. It's about 60 miles of interesting cliffs, with lots of whales. We haven't time to make the trip, unfortunately. He had read about us in the Quebec paper. I shower and shave and off we go to Harold Price's. It's an old ramshackle place with posts placed at strategic locations to bolster the sagging ceiling. An older couple, Lewis and Betty Evans, are there. We have a nice evening. Harold provides wine and smoked oysters. Mr. Evans places his house and car at our disposal. Harold sent someone to the boat to splice our lines. Very good job.

Harold Price's home, known as the Pilot House, is strategically sit-
uated at the mouth of the Saguenay. Carolann denied that it was
"ramshackle," describing it instead as "quaint." Price was one of the
most memorable people the crew met as they sailed up the north
coast. His family had a long history in Tadoussac, and Price told them
stories and offered information that made them feel knowledgeable
about the area. At the time they met Price, he was recovering from
heart surgery, and the crew enjoyed his perspective on life. In many
ways, sailing north aboard *Aqua Star* was their way of living life to
the fullest, and in Harold Price they met a man who could appreciate that choice.

Waiting out another spell of heavy weather in Tadoussac before
moving on to the next lower St. Lawrence port of Baie Comeau,
Carolann and Gay took the Evanses up on their offer of baths, while
David and Leslie visited a restaurant and indulged in coffee, apple
pie, and conversation.

A northeast wind, the worst kind, is strengthening, with horizontal rain. Clouds lower and obscure the surrounding hilltops.
This is a very lovely area and we are disappointed about the
weather. I wanted to get some footage—it's so pretty—but only
about two or three slides. Leslie has said again he wants me to
sail with him and even live on board. I enjoy his company and
find his thought processes quite interesting.

The wind is howling through the rigging and we rock gently in the protection of the harbor. We see sea urchins clinging
to the rocks just below the surface at low tide. At high tide, of
course, they are too deep to be seen. At this time, 4:30 P.M., we
aren't sure when we shall leave for Baie Comeau, but I suspect
we will be up at 3 A.M.

Baie Comeau is an evocative name for many Canadians. It is a fac-
tory town and has a reputation for being close-knit. As the con-
stituency of Canada's former prime minister, Brian Mulroney, it
achieved some notoriety. For the crew of *Aqua Star,* the welcome they
received at Baie Comeau was a low point of the voyage. Here's how
Leslie tells it:

At 8 P.M. we entered the harbor at Baie Comeau and headed toward Club Nautique. As we approached the docks, we saw a lot of people standing around, but no one helped to make room for us to tie up. All they had to do was move a small fishing boat, but they just stood there. We had no choice but to back out. We were exhausted, having sailed since 4 A.M. We couldn't continue, as I did not plot the course—I was going to do that here, tomorrow. We tried to find a place to anchor...by now it was dark. We dropped the hook in the harbor entrance (not in the way of traffic), but big swells came at us and the rolling was unbearable. I had the riding sails up, but not even a breeze, so *Aqua Star* was beam-to the swells. We picked up the anchor and motored around the harbor until we found a big steel barge covered with mud which we managed to tie up to. We were all so exhausted after this evening we didn't feel like eating...just sleeping. In my miserable state I joked, "This is probably the barge that leaves at 6 o'clock in the morning!" I wondered, after all the human kindness we had experienced, why had this happened here? Without any effort, we all fell asleep.

At 7:45 A.M. I was wakened, but not by the alarm. I heard a motor. A big motor sound. Quickly I stuck my head up through the hatch and saw this humongous tugboat tying up to the barge. Everything was shaking and moving. I called to them to wait a minute. I ran through the boat yelling for everyone to get up—get dressed. Immediately I started the engine, but by this time one of them had untied our stern line. Gay jumped onto the barge to fend off the clipper bow. The stern then drifted out so far I thought she would not be able to get back on board. We managed to get safely away, but I was mad. I hated this place so much, I immediately pumped out right in the harbor.

We found a rough concrete wall across the harbor to tie up to long enough to get out the charts and plot the course to Sept-Iles.

I made espresso coffee for the first time since we left Toronto. Gay claimed the espresso stopped her headache instantly, but I think she would just like to have it more often. By 6 P.M. we were on our way and heading toward Sept-Iles. We sailed all night—it was beautiful. The sea was full of phosphorus. I picked up a bucketful and played with it in the cockpit. The wind died and we motored again. In the middle of the night the engine alarm came on. I was up like a bullet and killed the engine. After investigating, I discovered the saltwater impeller had disintegrated. I went to my engine spares, found a new one which I put on, and in less than three hours we were underway again . . . Crisis number 2.

Everyone was affected by the coldness of Baie Comeau's welcome. Leslie plotted their course to Sept-Iles, their next port of call near Anticosti Island, where the St. Lawrence River widens into the Gulf of St. Lawrence. Meanwhile, Carolann tackled David on the subject of water conservation: She demanded that he stop using half a cup of water to brush his teeth. In order to prepare the crew for the hardships to come on the Labrador Coast, and to conserve difficult-to-obtain fresh water, Leslie had requested that salt water should be used for everything but drinking and cooking. Carolann suspected David of ignoring the captain's request, and Leslie eventually cut off the water supply to the aft cabin to prevent the incorrigibly clean David from using fresh water.

At Baie Comeau, Carolann stopped writing regularly. She was no longer able to write under sail, and was taking four Gravol pills each day to combat nausea. Although she was never sleepy because of them, and never missed her watches, she did think they made her melancholy. She was angry with David, as well as Leslie because somehow his being there meant that Leslie had a pal on board. She was sickened by all of the male bonding that was going on, although the most serious complaints she had with David were that he used fresh water to brush his teeth and hadn't brought the best type of camera equipment to make the all-important film record of the voyage. She actually found ways to be angry at David on Leslie's behalf. Leslie, on the other hand, treated David with kid gloves:

Leslie always wants us to conserve battery power on board, and tells us never to leave lights on unnecessarily. We had all gone to bed, except Leslie, who was completing some navigation for the next day and doing his routine maintenance checks. When eventually he went to the aft cabin he discovered David in his bunk with the light on. He said, "Boy, you must be a light sleeper!" That's how Leslie reprimands David—quite a contrast with the method he uses with me and Gay.

Carolann kept busy when *Aqua Star* was in port, took walks alone or with Gay, and tried hard to keep calm.

In Gay, Carolann had an ally in mistrusting David:

> I'm growing tired of "the boys"—again it happens that I must push to learn. Leslie always addresses David re navigation, plans, engine, etc. David gobbles this up. I will not be pushed out because I'm female!
>
> I snapped at David today because he's so crafty and needs to be more rugged and rough. More or less told him to butt out. He gets under my skin 'cause I'm afraid with his keen, keen, keen to learn, I'll be neglected. He bloody well comes out of this with a film. Me, I'll only be a better sailor, but I must be included and given priority to learn. I will have a little talk with Leslie in Sept-Iles when I get him alone. David is now sulking and lying low—shame. I'm not yet sorry.
>
> Someone keeps going off course at the helm and I know it's not me because I really aim for accuracy no matter what wind and sea conditions may be. Cannot understand it. I'm going to watch everyone from now on—I don't like being blamed for what I'm not guilty of!

Accuracy on the helm was a sore point with Gay and Carolann. They were on the firing line when *Aqua Star* was off course, while they both thought privately that since David was so busy enjoying the scenery when he was at the helm that the deviations were his. Leslie even told Carolann that according to his plotting, her watches were best for accuracy. But the warnings about staying on course were delivered to the crew as a whole.

Meanwhile, David was almost oblivious of the tempests he was causing:

Carolann and Gay on watch. Watches were generally four hours on, four hours off.

I do dishes on aft deck with Carolann. I ask a question of Gay. I think she misinterprets it and flies off. A most spoiled, immature child.

Gay was determined that The First Canadian Sub-Arctic Sailing Expedition was going to be her claim to fame. Increasingly, she was grasping for ways to make use of the journey to improve her status, to help her establish herself. From the beginning she had planned to write a cookbook, publish her diary, make use of her public relations contacts—perhaps even become a long-distance passagemaker in her own right. She began to think of experiences and people she met as a kind of personal inventory:

If the weather permits tomorrow, we plan to sail *Aqua Star* like mad so that David can film. I hope I can be shown in the film doing all hard sailwork for the exposure as a serious sailor. I realize I'm learning a lot bit by bit. Matt will be proud of me. I'm proud of me.

I've written postcards, I've updated my journal—hope I

haven't neglected to document any important observations. Hope I can bloody turn this daily scribble into a best seller! I have been thinking of an angle, and I think I'd be most comfortable with my genuine struggle to become, be accepted, be determined enough to be, a sailor. Anything less personal may be boring or become fiction. We'll see. Something I must continue to think about, though.

At Sept-Iles, the weather kept them in port for six days. David noted that "the area is rougher, the boats tougher, and weather gruffer," as they moved out of the river. But the welcome in Sept-Iles was warm. One evening, they were invited for dinner aboard a nearby fishing vessel.

> Leslie, Carolann, Gay, and I were guests of Maurice, Jean-Pierre, and Pierre—a most congenial and fun group. Very nice evening. Leslie left early to plot courses. He is very anxious to be away tomorrow around 10 A.M. I've never seen Carolann so relaxed—she's flying. At the party she was quite flirty and had a wonderful time.

Gay briefly noted that something had happened at the dinner:

> Lots of festivities.
> Leslie voiced his disgust and humiliation re dinner party on fishing vessel. Voiced also his hate. Carolann disappeared not understanding why he is accusing her. Oh dear, this must all blow over or we will not make it.

The whole story came out the next day in David's journal:

> When Leslie turned off his alarm and went back to sleep, I knew we wouldn't be leaving today. Leslie went out in the wind and rain. We had breakfast of eggs and chicken livers. I fought my way to the post office and mailed off films and letters. Leslie came in and is very upset, told Carolann he was very embarrassed by her actions at the party, about her feeling Pierre's leg, and things she said. Leslie says he hates her and he will rid him-

self of her and sell *Aqua Star* after this expedition. He leaves. Carolann leaves. Gay and I discuss and agree this is not good for the expedition. Leslie has a strong will and is serious, we are sure. He never says anything he doesn't mean, and we know how it bothers him to be made fun of or degraded or made to look foolish. He hates it.

We've had four days of very strong, steady east winds. Today there is fog. We are told the ice is blowing in and is four inches thick and solid 150 miles from here. We can only sit and wait for the wind to change. We look across the raging waters to an island some six kilometers away. Even at this distance we can see the 10-meter waves climbing up and smashing in white foam on its rocky shoreline. Leslie is worried about the dock *AS* is tied to. As I sit here in the clubhouse, I can see both *AS* and the dock moving back and forth over a two-meter range. The rain is horizontal. I have worn my wet clothes and carried my wet sweater and watch cap over here and spread them on chairs to dry out. I feel I must make a purchase to justify the space I'm taking and order a coffee and leave $1 on her tray. I don't want the coffee. Leslie sits down and talks about putting the 9.9hp motor on the Zodiac and beating our way over to the island to get pictures of the 30-foot waves and the surf. I'm kind of inclined to go, but the discomforts win out. We'd be soaked in salt water (and it never dries). Very cold, cutting rain, seasick tossing around in waves, but most important, I would not be able to shoot movies or even to take still pictures—cameras would be soaked. Not worth it, I decide. Dance at the marina.

The incident of Pierre's leg was a classic piece of misinterpretation. Carolann was sitting on the settee in *Aqua Star*'s cabin next to Pierre. The others were also sitting around the table, and the table concealed everyone below the waist. Here's Carolann's side of the story:

Pierre was sitting on the edge of the settee, and he said that he couldn't bend his leg at the knee. He was telling us about this and making a joke. We were all laughing and having fun. I grabbed his other knee and said, "Is this one stiff too?" We laughed. But Leslie wasn't in the mood for fun. It was the pressure of the voyage. Under normal circumstances, Leslie would never have blown a situation like this out of proportion.

Whatever the tensions on board, the expedition was now truly off the beaten path. The ports were farther apart and sparsely settled. *Aqua Star* was lucky to find a berth at the rough town docks and often ended up anchoring in the fishing harbors where they now put in for water and fuel.

Soon the harbors changed from towns to tiny outports and settlements. Originally these harbors were active fishing ports, and even today they exist along these harsh shores because of the fishing industry, despite its continued decline over many decades.

With the increasing harshness of the weather, *Aqua Star*'s crew began to feel the demands of hard sailing and long passages. They recognized that interpersonal conflict had to be swept aside in order for them to meet the even harder sailing ahead.

But when *Aqua Star* left Sept-Iles for Mingan, 75 nautical miles closer to the Strait of Belle Isle, the weather brightened, although the atmosphere on board kept worsening. Leslie only talked to David; Carolann stayed away from the men, even at mealtimes—not an easy thing to do on the yacht. Still, David and Leslie had a pleasant time together, and David's journal recorded fishing and joking with him. At Mingan, they discovered that once again the government guide promised more than the facilities delivered. They explored the beach and fished, taking a short break from the boat, then sailed on to Havre St. Pierre, where they anchored overnight.

Sailing for Natashquan the next day, Carolann and Gay talked to David about Leslie.

Gay didn't expect a dictatorial captain who constantly puts women down—treats them as stupid animals. He treats me fairly, although I won't discuss any of his decisions anymore. He is the captain and I do as he says. He is not always correct. The girls, especially Carolann, take terrible verbal abuse, and are constantly humiliated in front of anyone—even on land.

Our charts are excellent, except that they do not have details now of the shoreline. They are designed for the big ships with shipping lanes quite a distance from shore.

The waves get larger. By midafternoon the sea has become very rough. Communication between all parties is practically nonexistent. I decide to shake them up. I write a letter of resignation: I want off at the next stop.

Desperate situations demand desperate measures. It works, if only temporarily. Now their attention as a group is directed at me, and they are talking as a group, a team. We talk it out and everything is much better.

We see a whale leaping straight up in the air full-length and then smashing down in a mound of spray and white foam. He repeats it about six times.

David handed his letter of resignation to Carolann, instead of Leslie, leaving her once again caught in the middle. On reading the letter, Carolann threw questions and accusations at David. "I told him I didn't care whether he stayed or not, but that for Leslie's sake, he'd better. Leslie was counting on a film being made." Carolann declared to Gay that it was a sign of David's manipulative nature. He had told her casually one day that he had a talent for manipulating people. Leslie blamed Carolann. Everyone, as David said, at least used his letter as an excuse to clear the air and re-focus on the expedition.

It was a fortuitous time for clearing the air, because their next port of call offered them all a chance to relax and enjoy the luxurious hospitality of Captain Tony—a larger-than-life personality who became their host in the fishing port of Natashquan.

We arrive at Natashquan. The approach is full of shoals. We take in our sails and ready for either tie-up or anchoring. We approach cautiously, with Leslie constantly checking the chart, and we all look for markers. Under the most severe conditions to date, we do get in and the anchor is dropped. Gay, Leslie, and I take the Zodiac and fishermen signal for us to raft beside them. We are an oddity in this outpost. We inquire from a fisherman about the purchase of a fish for supper. He takes us toward a Portuguese fish-processing ship and somehow we end up in the captain's cabin. We talk over a bottle of fine Portuguese red wine. The fisherman is ignored but after an embarrassing length of time, the captain finally produces a bottle of brandy for him.

Carl, the government agent, asks me if I'd like a shower and gives me gear, bless him.

The fisherman shows no restraint and shortly is falling off his seat. We are invited back for an inspection of the fish processing and lunch tomorrow. A very interesting evening. We return to *Aqua Star* and settle for a ham sandwich. We are very tired after a tough day. The fish the captain gave us will be cooked for breakfast.

We sleep well and late, no doubt assisted by the rocking of *Aqua Star* at anchor. I cleaned the fish and Gay poached it in a pot of water with garlic. Neither did the fish justice, and some that was served was still raw. And I ended up doing last night's supper dishes as well as this morning's.

We Zodiac over to the processing ship but arrive at 1:20, their break period. We sneaked off in the Zodiac and put in at the dock. Where we tied up, floating on its back, is a dead seal—a beautiful creature. We hitch a ride on the back of a pick-up truck and bounce into town, about one mile. We pick up wine and munchies, expecting to have the other captain on board this evening.

I got to wash my face with soap and fresh water in the restaurant. I'd relish a shower. We receive word that the processing ship's captain is expecting us for supper. Wow. All kinds of wines, everything. We start with cold platter, then soup, then the entreé. We are at the officer's table—a long table with about 14 of us around it. The cook, who never smiles, serves us in the most correct manner. Desserts are gorgeous, with brandy, cognac, wines, etc.

Later, on the processing ship we are served steaks with eggs and coffee. Gay and I stay, Leslie and Carolann go back to *Aqua Star*. Gay and I and Captain Tony talk till 6:30 a.m. Tony goes away. Gay sleeps in his bed. I sleep on the couch till 9 a.m., dress, go to the bridge, and film fishing boats unloading.

Boats are from all around the area, not from Natashquan.

The Portuguese ship took
on cod from fishing boats
that arrived daily to have
their catches transferred,
weighed, cleaned and salted away in her hold.

They average 8,000 lbs. of fish per day. The boat has over one million lbs. salted away. Tony and crew are Portuguese. They do two trips a year and make enough money to holiday the other six months. A full load of cod is 3 million lbs. The fishermen use gill nets three inches wide. They gut the fish as they come into harbor. The processing ship takes them aboard in nets with a weight scale attached. The fish are dumped on the deck. A fish is then beheaded over a board. The heads are then cut up for tongues and lower jaws. The rest of the head is discarded. The body is sliced and part of the backbone removed. It then goes into the ship's hold, where each piece is salted and stacked three feet high in long rows. A blanket of sacking is rolled over it and another row started. The salt, brought from Portugal, removes moisture. A Crown corporation, The Saltfish Co-op, has two representatives on board (Carl and Jack) who grade and weigh the fish and pay the fishermen. The ship's captain then pays the co-op. About 24 fishing boats are supplying the fish.

To pick up my camera from *Aqua Star*, the captain insists we take an orange-colored lifeboat as big as *Aqua Star*. Two guys crank the engine, hit it with a rusty shovel, and it goes faster.

After a few short weeks of their own company aboard *Aqua Star*, the crew all relished the company of Captain Tony—and the change of routine he provided them.

CHAPTER SEVEN

✣

NATASHQUAN TO
GOOSE BAY

*A*qua Star arrived at Natashquan on June 28. On July 1, she left port after 48 hours of Portuguese hospitality, music, and dancing, courtesy of "Captain Tony." Captain Tony sent the crew off with a great box of supplies, including liqueurs for Carolann and Gay. Leslie was becoming concerned that his crew would forget the expedition in their enjoyment of the luxury and happy company. He made a point of lightening the atmosphere as they sailed that day, making a short trip to Kegashka, where they anchored overnight.

The route to Blanc Sablon, on the Quebec–Labrador border, was more challenging. The crew sighted their first iceberg. Rocks and shoals, ice and fog meant that *Aqua Star* moved carefully, and they watched the depthsounder constantly. Icebergs and a change from fresh to freeze-dried food and boil bags were the day's milestones for David:

> The iceberg, brilliant white against the gray-black water, appears to be hung up on the shoreline. We just passed very close to some islands, so we are altering course to 125 degrees to increase the distance from land. The iceberg has us worried, too.

Tonight when it's dark, we will slow from our usual five knots down to two knots. *Aqua Star* will rupture if we hit ice at a faster speed. When it storms, we head out. It's the shoreline, rocks, and islands that can wreck us.

We now start on the Magic Pantry and Hardee Freeze-Dried dinners. They may not be great, but neither is Gay's cooking. One morning for breakfast we had Cream of Wheat that she had cooked the night before. Cold and gooey. Yuck. Gay tried making french fries. Her method is to put the chips in the grease and then put the pot on the stove. I don't believe the grease ever did get up to temperature. The chips became a gooey mass that soaked up most of the grease and then stuck to the bottom of the pot. The other day I cleaned three cod that the Portuguese had given us. Gay made a broth and cooked them in it with a lot of garlic. I couldn't taste the fish for garlic. Perhaps it's just as well, as it was raw anyway. She cooks most everything in a lot of oil and uses tons of herbs. I think she believes this is exotic cooking. I tried to show her once how to make bacon and eggs and she flew off. She tells me things thinking she is educating me. Like most young people, she is just discovering things and thinks it's new for everyone. Consequently, she is quite boring but thinks she's very knowledgeable and cultured.

To do Gay justice, she offered the crew a variety of meals, was seldom late with them, and often was not given enough time to finish her own meal after serving the others before she was required to move to get underway. Meeting the Portuguese captain had put a new interest in the voyage for Gay. Her flirtations were more grist for the personality-development mill that was The First Canadian Sub-Arctic Sailing Expedition.

Hope I see the Portuguese ship again—I love being spoiled like that. Captain Tony and I discussed love till 6 A.M. only two days ago and I'm really considering some things he said. . . .

I wonder if I should leave Canada, emigrate to Europe, and marry an older man. . . .

Frozen delight. The blue streaks in the icebergs are crevices that fill with melted water then freeze closed once again.

The port of Blanc Sablon was Aqua Star's *last stop before the Strait of Belle Isle.*

Blanc Sablon is French on one side, English on the other. A ferry runs from there to Newfoundland, and the port is near the entrance to the perilous Strait of Belle Isle. Leslie waited in Blanc Sablon two days for the most auspicious weather before entering the strait.

We moved over to the public wharf, where I telephoned for a fuel truck. We topped up our water also. Just as I was going below, somebody called, "Hey skipper! There's another sailboat in the harbor!" What? I popped my head up, and sure thing, and it is no small boat either. I don't like this. What if somebody is trying to beat me out of being the first sailing yacht to Churchill? This happened a few years back when *Bernier II* tried to be the first sailboat to go through the Northwest Passage. Captain Real then found himself in a race with Willy De Roos, from Belgium, and *Bernier II* lost. It took Real three years to get through, but Willy De Roos made it in one season. I just now realized, we haven't seen any sailboat since we left Montreal, so I have a good excuse to go over and talk to the skipper, because I am sure he too needs fuel—I'll tell him the truck will be here in an hour.

As I got closer, I could see the Canadian flag and that she was from Quebec and her name was *Moby Dick*. Then I met her captain, Richard Drouin, his wife Marthe, and their two teenage daughters, who were on their way to Greenland. A big sigh of relief ... this was not competition, but a fellow Arctic sailor. He told me he was leaving tomorrow, Friday (I guess he's not superstitious like me—I wouldn't leave anywhere on a Friday). Besides, I was hoping for a clear day to enter the Strait of Belle Isle. But, after talking to the locals, who claim this to be the foggiest place on earth—one shouldn't wait around for sunshine. I had butterflies in my stomach because there were two places on this expedition which have kept me awake many nights in the past four years—one the Strait of Belle Isle, the other the Hudson Strait.

The Strait of Belle Isle can get very nasty. If a northeast storm blows, the whole Atlantic Ocean tries to squeeze through the narrow strait, which is only nine miles across at its narrowest point. The seas can build to a very dangerous and destructive

Fishing boats on the Labrador aren't deterred by fog; they leave port at 5 A.M. daily to tend their nets, often relying on radar.

height. Add to this the fog, the constant presence of ice, and the shipping traffic, and you have the perfect sailor's nightmare.

In Blanc Sablon, a couple of French Canadian divers working on a Parks Canada project enjoyed some of Carolann's Hungarian fishhead soup and invited the crew to take showers at their motel. Leslie and Carolann took the ferry to St. Barbe, Newfoundland, to bring back a bottle of the potent Newfoundland liquor known as Screech, while Gay and David guarded *Aqua Star.* Gay spent more time with the divers:

> David drove Leslie and Carolann to the ferry just in time. I stayed behind because Claudy and Marcel arrived in their dinghies to wish us *Salut!* Lovely. They stayed briefly for coffee and were very free with their comments and impressions of each of us. David: uncommunicative (true). He's so quiet in social situations. Carolann and I would be fun to meet in different circumstances. True. We'd have a ball! Claudy will not forget my face ever in his whole life. Hope we all meet again.
>
> I did no work today. Chatted with David re male and female capabilities. David is quite generous and rational but he still slips up through breeding—he refers to Carolann and me as "gals."

Aqua Star's next destination was Red Bay, site of an underwater archaeological dig for the remains of a fifteenth-century Basque vessel and settlement. It's the halfway point in the Strait of Belle Isle, and the ice warnings were ominous. In spite of fog, they got underway in order to avoid being kept in port by worse weather predicted for the next day. David described the preparations aboard *Aqua Star* for leaving Blanc Sablon:

> Up at 6:30. A wall of fog encircles the boat. Leslie changed the oil in the motor last night. It's a very still morning. The boat is rocking ever so gently. I stay, dressed, in the aft cabin, writing in my log. Leslie is going over the charts—we head for Red Bay about 80 km away. I hear him say to Gay, "I can't even see

the bow." Gay wakens very slowly and prefers not to be pushed or even spoken to for the first hour. Carolann busies herself in the early morning but walks about sleepily, hanging onto the warmth and comfort she has just given up. I dress, then change my mind, undress, and put on longjohns first, white athletic socks, a favorite heavy yellow sweater, then my down vest, which I wear a great deal. I'll be putting on my white raingear later, as everything outside is drenched. I know the dense fog will creep inside our clothes and we will soon be shivering. My hands and feet are already cold. My breath is a mist here in the aft cabin. Yesterday we were told that the water temperature is 31°F or 0°Celsius. Warm air over the cold water causes the fog.

The weather radio informs us that the Strait of Belle Isle has considerable old ice, bergy bits, and a fair number of icebergs. We learn that the ice is the worst in 10 years. Ships aren't getting up north; fishermen aren't getting out and fish are three weeks late in appearing. Poor visibility and fog. The report then lists the lights that are out and we hear the winter spar lifting [adjusting and replacing marks shifted by winter storms and ice] is still in progress. Only the larger icebergs will show on the radar, so we will have to proceed very slowly in this fog. All eyes will be watching. Icebergs aren't as much of a threat as the pack ice, which can encircle us. We could also go down an alley of open water between ice strips and find ourselves in a dead end. We can also expect rain.

I look out the portlight. A most inhospitable environment. I hear the girls topside doing yesterday's dishes. This isn't very pleasant, for we scoop our dishwater from overboard and the ice water quickly numbs the hands. As we cast off, we are amazed to see the shoreline. The fog has lifted. As we proceed out of the harbor, the sky becomes blue above while we have only 300 meters of visibility around us. The fog is like a 30-foot-high wall of cotton batting all around. We proceed cautiously, the foghorn warning us to post a lookout on the bow. One hour later, the fog has cleared and we motorsail in sunshine.

I take time now to go over all my photo and sound equipment. The electronic camera has a brown powder inside. Uh-oh.

David counted 41 icebergs on one of his watches. To photograph one iceberg, Gay rowed David close to it in the inflatable. While they were shooting, a section of the berg broke away, thundering into the sea. Leslie maneuvered Aqua Star *between the resulting waves and the inflatable. Even so, David and Gay had a short, wild ride in the deep, icy water.*

I clean thoroughly but wonder about the 400-foot roll of film that just passed through, which is reel #421. As we proceed to Red Bay, we see parcels of snow in the hills along the northern coast about four miles away. Our Omega was erratic before Leslie grounded it. Now it works fine, showing us our position. The SatNav verifies it. The radio contact has now been established. Edmonton had picked us up but we were not able to raise Halifax until this morning. It comes in poorly, however.

Leslie and Gay are friendly but Carolann is very cool, answering only curtly if I address her. If I make a statement, she is very quick to point out it can't possibly be so, I am definitely wrong. I believe it's because Leslie and I communicate so very well and Carolann can't communicate with Leslie. She resents my intrusion between them.

I spent a good part of the day working on my equipment, wiping it with cloth dampened with fresh water, cleaning lenses, changing the conversion filter in the electric, and working on broken shorting-out cable. We passed an iceberg on the port side and got a good photo and movies.

As we entered Red Bay, water and wind got quite rough. We anchored and dinghied to pier to shop in the only two stores. Later the others went off again while I worked on equipment. They came back all excited about encounters with archaeological diggers. Guess I'll find out about it tomorrow.

They brought back a salmon, which I baked in the oven. It turned out well and we filmed the occasion using a fish-eye lens and lantern light.

I'm writing this in my bunk. The others have gone to a party. I didn't go because I had a 400-foot film magazine change to make and also tried to repair a cable, but I need Les to help hold parts. I heard them come in but I had no idea what time it was. I fell back into a sound sleep.

The next day's passage to Chateau Bay was a special one. In spite of wind and rain, when *Aqua Star* entered the bay's calm waters, the peace and grandeur of the place touched everyone. As they dropped anchor, a black bear foraging on shore was startled into the woods. Carolann said it was Shangri-la. *Aqua Star* overnighted in silence and tranquility, and her crew left the bay the next morning refreshed by it, as Carolann recorded:

Had a quiet and lengthy breakfast, the first while overnight stopping since we started. Waiting for the fog to lift. It was rather sad having to say good-bye to this lovely place, but I shall keep it tucked away in my memory for those special times in the years ahead when I wish to go traveling and can't—except in my thoughts.

The scenery gets even more beautiful—rugged, desolate, and intriguing. I have butterflies in my stomach I'm so excited. I want to laugh out loud and jump up and down and tell the whole world that life is wonderful, beautiful, and exciting if you

Icebergs, 86 per cent underwater, can even gouge ruts in the ocean floor. Fresh water runs off as the ice above water level melts. Erosion by waves and melting sculpts the older bergs into fantastic shapes until they finally collapse and topple over.

really live it. I'm so thankful that I am having this opportunity to participate in this adventure. We are just beginning now to see the wonders of Mother Nature here in the Labrador.

It was July 8, and one of Leslie's nightmare passages, the Strait of Belle Isle, was almost complete. David wrote that it was more memorable for its beauty than its treachery:

Heading out to sea, we can count seven icebergs. There is open water between *Aqua Star* and England and the swells roll the ship from one side to the other. We all feel a little queasy. A small black supply ship passes us and turns into a small settlement. Fishing boats pull up to it to collect their provisions. The black ship passes us again on its way to the next cluster of houses. We feel the air turn cold as we skirt an iceberg. The swells smash against it, spray flying, and we feel the boom each time.

We are in awe of the beauty in the color and contours. As we make the turn northward around the tip of Labrador, we navigate cautiously, islands and shoals all around us. We are in calm, protected waters. Our flags hang limp. We are very content and happy, reveling in the harsh, immense loveliness.

Gay rows me ashore in the Zodiac, where I set up my cameras. Leslie and Carolann motor *Aqua Star* past a beautifully colored and shaped bergy bit as I shoot 100 feet of film and eight slides. Veins of dark blue run through the pale blue bergs. We pull into Fox Harbour and tie up to a great new wharf. I talk with a big, affable Newfoundlander. He is very happy. He explains that today is his first day at work. He has just been hired by the government fish station. His wife teaches school here. So their future is assured. The Labrador community here resent his getting the job; they consider him an outsider. But no one here was qualified for the job, he explains.

Only one sailboat came here last year, he tells us, and we could very well be the only one this year. Probably every house has a pair of binoculars trained on us right now. And, when he gets home, they will all be phoning him to find out about us. Anything from the outside is big news.

We walk a mile to the grocery store, fighting huge mosquitoes every foot of the way. We buy goodies: potato chips, pop, cookies. I get half a dozen Pepsis—it seems I'm always thirsty. [David wore Transderm patches to prevent seasickness; one of their side effects is a dry mouth.] We visit the clinic (hospital) and we can have a hot bath there. Pauline, the nurse, is a very nice young lady. Originally from Kingston, she talks about the simple life and how it grows on you. She has a cook, a nurse's aide, and a maintenance man. A doctor visits every six weeks, a dentist every four months. The people here have their teeth pulled for $10. They can't afford $40 for a filling.

A gravel airstrip is being built beside the clinic. Mud and rocks are everywhere.

In spite of the isolation of the Labrador Coast, *Aqua Star* was very much in touch with the outside world. Via single-sideband radio through Polestar, courtesy of Canterra, they sent messages to the media. They called home from homes and stores in port, enjoying the chance to talk to people not caught up in the introspection and self-absorption of the *Aqua Star* crew themselves. They telephoned me in Toronto from Fox Harbour, full of stories about the milk of human kindness, the generosity of the people they were meeting, and the beauty of the country. No mention of the tensions on board that were at the tops of their minds only days earlier.

They even did television and radio interviews. Leslie, as captain, did the talking, which was a little frustrating for Gay and Carolann, who were eager to express themselves. Interviewers who tried to elicit an unrehearsed remark from Leslie were also frustrated when he seemed determined to stick to standard phrases such as, "Our goal is to promote the Canadian spirit of adventure and our seafaring heritage. . . . *Aqua Star* takes the maple leaf to places it has never been."

In a radio interview from Goose Bay, Labrador, Erika Ritter, on her CBC program, "Day Shift," asked Leslie if he had found that life on board had changed anyone's personality:

"I think mine changed for the worse. But you have to be very flexible. At the beginning of the trip, there was a bit of friction between us, but later on, by the time we reached Quebec City, we all settled in and everything since has gone smoothly. . . ."

Leslie would refuse to admit that life on board was a hurly-burly of tension relieved by moments of excitement and wonder. It seemed that whenever the pressure of sailing hard let up, the crew had time for friction and temper. For a few days, sailing for Groswater Bay, the entrance to Hamilton Inlet, they were all busy concentrating on their jobs and the constant danger of pack ice.

Aqua Star was making good progress. Her stuffing box was leaking again, her speed impeller had been sheared off by ice, and Leslie was concerned about a potential problem with the propeller shaft, but each day's run was bringing them 80 or 90 nautical miles closer to the Goose Bay NATO base and the repair facilities they might need. Spirits were generally good. Gay had decided that she should keep her nose to the grindstone and stop being a brat:

> Beautiful sunny day. Take lots of film and photos of blue icebergs 150 to 200 feet high. David and I were in the dinghy

When a storm approached over the water, said David, "it could be seen in time for the crew to don foul weather gear and prepare for the buckets of icy water that would soon be running down our necks and into the boat."

The crew of Aqua Star *was in awe of the natural beauty around them, relishing everything from dramatic weather changes to delicate wildflowers.*

Icebergs constantly enthralled the crew on the Labrador Coast passage.

while *Aqua Star* sailed past. Exciting and dangerous. I now consider myself brave.

I work hard on board most of the time.

We averaged about six knots today, traveling 91 nautical miles! Progress made us all happy. We managed to anchor near Domino Harbour by nightfall. There's a lot of ice and bergs on the horizon. Hope we don't get delayed for weeks.

Sometimes I really enjoy my shifts at the helm. Leslie often tells us, "Keep accurate." Sometimes that's not easy. Everyone is defensive. I do notice that I like it less now that the one-hour shifts are rigid. That's my problem, but I've tried to figure out what makes the others like the discipline.

Fairness is another topic I must include in my journal somewhere. Those who preach it don't always practice! Carolann lectured me about my diet in the supermarket and she's ending up to be so different—rarely eats what I cook the others, fixes things for herself or eats at different times. She has also rearranged a lot of the provisions and when asked why, has no healthy explanations. Quite frankly, I find her very competitive with me, but in a friendly way. What I don't understand is why the interest is shown now. I'll just go my merry way—I must reach Churchill sane!

Good motorsail—I really love the days when I'm totally involved in the navigation. Progress means so much more. Wind strong from the west. Ran into lots of pack ice. Floated all night in Groswater Bay. Leslie is tired; he stayed up all night. Rain. No ships. We will be into Rigolet by noon Friday.

Carolann, in fact, was unable to eat anything but the most bland foods—biscuits, bread, and porridge. And she did rearrange the storage of foods that Gay was eating to make them less accessible. This problem with food came as a surprise to Carolann—she'd read about crews fighting over food but never really believed it could happen on *Aqua Star.*

In Rigolet, at the entrance to Hamilton Inlet—which is in turn the Atlantic Coast entrance to Lake Melville and Goose Bay—David and Leslie spent part of the afternoon chasing a killer whale, which outwitted them as they tried to maneuver for a good camera angle. Carolann and Gay had a companionable drink, followed by another of Gay's outbursts. For a change, David found himself on the defensive:

Gay has had a few drinks and has thrown a tantrum. I ignore it. Carolann won't let it pass and she and Gay have a 15-minute argument. Carolann then jumps on me for not standing up for myself. Carolann thinks that she is the only normal person on board and that the rest of us are weird.

As Gay herself noted, "it never stops." Four people in close quarters was a recipe for aggravation. None of the tensions ever received mention in Leslie's diary. Carolann was convinced that her marriage was ending. David was content to calm things when he could but otherwise chose to keep quiet and enjoy the scenery. And Gay had decided that her policy would be to get away from *Aqua Star* at every opportunity, take her pleasures where she found them, and get to Churchill as fast as she could.

CHAPTER EIGHT

✳

GOOSE BAY TO
MAKKOVIK

The difference between the weather in Groswater Bay and that in Lake Melville has been described as "like passing from winter into summer." *Aqua Star*'s passage through Hamilton Inlet, however, was not so pleasant.

Sailing through the inlet on the approach to Goose Bay about 40 miles inland, winds reached 40 knots, with a 2½-knot current. As night fell, so did a heavy rain. *Aqua Star* drifted in the pitch darkness of the river with two on watch and Leslie awake all night. The river was narrow and there were no markers, so they waited until dawn to get underway again. *Aqua Star* tacked back and forth to make some headway upriver. Finally, they anchored overnight in Lake Melville and sailed into Goose Bay's Terrington Basin early next morning.

All of the subsistence hunting and fishing that once was the way of life of the aboriginal people and European settlers in the Lake Melville region was subjugated to the war industry in 1942. The United States took a 99-year lease on the airfield, which provided air cover to transatlantic convoys during World War II. With the airfield came wage-labor work for those who had lived by fur trapping and fishing. Goose Bay became the home of the Strategic Air Command and its staff, while nearby Happy Valley received the influx of

Newfoundlanders, Cree and Inuit attracted by the newly booming economy. In the summer of 1985, Goose Bay was the dynamic NATO center for pilot testing and training on low-flying jets. American and British armed forces personnel and contractors still formed the economic base of the town, which has been struggling for decades to diversify its economy.

Arriving at the busy Terrington Basin docks, the crew of *Aqua Star* immediately returned to the pattern of port activity they had established in the St. Lawrence. They spent 10 days in Goose Bay—arranging for *Aqua Star*'s repairs, meeting dignitaries and interested locals, and enjoying Labrador hospitality.

They were offered showers on board a Coast Guard vessel and private cabins for a night on a supply ship moored nearby. A wealthy businessman and former Member of Provincial Parliament, Mel Woodward of Woodward Group, provided *Aqua Star*'s fuel on behalf

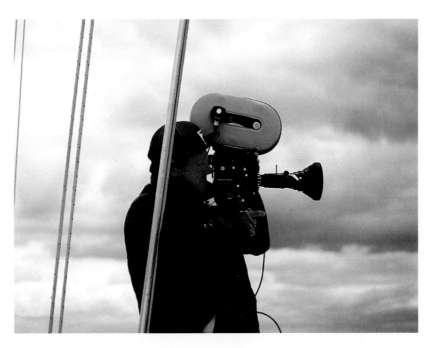

David Farr tackled the challenges of 16 millimeter photography in salt spray, in freezing temperatures, aboard a constantly moving platform.

of their sponsor, Canterra. He also arranged for transportation in
Goose Bay and took time to entertain the crew in grand style at his
home and in the town.

Once again, everyone had a glimpse of Leslie relaxed and full of
charm, without a care. Carolann delighted in his return to light-
heartedness. At Mel Woodward's home, he spent an evening dancing
to "Newfie boogie," as he called Newfoundland-style folk music.

The Felsberg family invited the Sikes to spend time with them at
their self-sufficient homestead on nearby Mud Lake. Susan Felsberg
had contacted the Sikes in Toronto and sent them background information about the Labrador. At Mud Lake, the Sikes were introduced
to caribou meat, and Carolann raved about its unusual, sweet flavor.

David kept busy on the *Aqua Star* film during the stay in Goose
Bay. Under sail, photography was a real problem. Gay and Carolann
constantly found fault with David because he was not ever-ready with
a camera. He often had to be reminded to film and seldom caught the
kind of exciting action and spontaneous footage they were hoping for.
But he was new to the problems of filming on a boat:

> I am frustrated with the cinematography. I would like to
> zoom in on subjects, but to zoom in increases apparent camera
> shake to the extent that the scenes would be unusable. Therefore
> I must content myself with wide-angle shots which make the
> subject very small. Even these are unusable many times because
> the ship is pitching and yawing and it throws me and the heavy
> camera in all directions. Often too, it's raining, or fog causes the
> lens to mist up.
>
> I'm anxious about the cameras, for in the hustle of changing
> cameras and lenses, taking light readings, focusing, and trying
> to keep the horizon level as we bob about, the equipment takes
> considerable bashing as it rolls back and forth in the bottom of
> the Zodiac with the sea water.

In port, however, David was always looking for photo opportuni-
ties. Although Carolann and Leslie had envisioned an adventure film
coming out of David's work on *Aqua Star,* David himself was more

familiar with the style and content of educational documentaries. The type of filming he was doing, particularly in the settlements *Aqua Star* visited, was designed for a travelogue rather than the sailing adventure Leslie had envisioned.

Both Gay and Carolann contrasted David's output with that of Matt Phillips. Working with CITY TV as a news "videographer" in Toronto, Matt's style was streetwise, full of action, made possible by Matt's own initiative and the type of equipment he was using. David's equipment was much less flexible, and David was more at home with scenic panoramas and static interviews.

I arise at 5:30 A.M. and drive around, taking pictures, still and movie. It's a beautiful, still morning. Back to *Aqua Star* at 8 A.M. Off to airport to check if parcel has arrived from Halifax. It contains the new housing and impeller for the damaged log. Leslie goes into one of his tirades at Carolann when she tries to get information from him about sending material to Judy Chopra and also picking up parcels. She does everything for him—butters his toast, fixes his coffee, looks up phone numbers, and though she patiently explains everything, he screams and rants.

At 10 A.M. we are cooked. The sun is very hot in the car, but the air outside is delightfully cool and dry.

We have visitors at *Aqua Star* almost constantly. The mayor comes and presents us with a Labrador flag for the boat. We passed a fishing boat in the channel on the way in here last week, the *Cathy Anne,* and talked with them on the radio. They promised us a sea trout dinner. Today they came over with four trout, cleaned them, and even supplied a cast-iron skillet and some fatback to oil it with. Gay cooked them and they are the best-tasting fish I've ever had.

We went bar-hopping in the base messes and the town. Then dinner at midnight at Mom's. Mel [Woodward] presented me with a beautiful collapsing fishing rod of graphite, complete with Mitchell reel and red devil lure. Also a small net. I promised to send him a picture of my first char. He asked that

I think of him whenever I use it. I'm really touched by his thoughtfulness.

Later, David put on SCUBA gear borrowed from Tex Arseneau (captain of the *Cathy Anne*) and dove to *Aqua Star*'s hull to replace the speed impeller, which had been repaired by Richard Felsberg.

Finally, *Aqua Star*'s overhaul was complete, and at 4 A.M. on July 21, she left the bustle of Goose Bay and again headed toward the Atlantic. The crew had had a summer holiday and were refreshed for the challenges of sailing north along the Labrador Coast. During this leg of the trip, ice warnings were frequent, settlements were few, and the waters often were uncharted. It was difficult now for *Aqua Star* to sail, and days would pass without the sails being raised. Under motor, six or seven knots was considered good speed. From Goose Bay on, provisions were harder to find and money to buy them was tight. The generosity of the people they met, however, delighted the crew and relieved the sense of deprivation they sometimes felt while sailing.

North of Goose Bay, the tiny communities welcome visitors warmly, letting them know it is "a real treat" when strangers stop by. Now that the sailing was colder, harder, and more dangerous, the crew of *Aqua Star* appreciated more than ever the cheerful hospitality they met everywhere.

Carolann reported to me on tape that there had been problems on board, but things were better and she felt that they had been the kinds of problems anyone would face on a cruise. She made the tape in Goose Bay, where Leslie had taken a holiday from his shipboard form. Like the 80°F temperatures they enjoyed in Goose Bay, Leslie's sunny mood while they were there was a much-needed respite. For Carolann, the break in Goose Bay had allowed her to freshen her outlook for the final push to Hudson Bay. But before they reached the coast near Rigolet, she was shadow-boxing with Leslie in her diary. She made note of a significant event. It was Day 64:

> For the first time I took the jib and main down myself without instruction or assistance (a great feeling). Tomorrow I'm going to put them up myself. Enough of this keeping me out of the picture. Of course, how can I know, do, or even have the

incentive if not encouraged, but pushed aside all the time and treated as if I'm different from the rest. I am as capable if not more so than Gay and David (for sure). I didn't have the time available in Toronto because I was working and doing the sponsors and promotion end of the expedition. I was always given the easiest jobs to do by Leslie. He has been the one person who has put me down and tried to keep me down and also at the same time the one who always criticizes and verbally abuses me for not knowing, but is least willing to instruct or give the opportunity to me to learn, and in this abusive way destroys my interest and incentive and I rebel. Who would react any differently?

But Carolann was still ready to fight for what she wanted:

Leslie and I are really making an effort to become close—like before all this expedition business started (another growing stage in our lives, but too bad this had to be part of Gay's and David's. They don't understand the commitment we have to each other and our determination in things we have committed ourselves to).

By this time, the crew harbored few illusions about their captain. David even had a few words to say in the privacy of his journal about *Aqua Star*'s design:

Leslie has built discomfort into *Aqua Star*. His reasoning is that we will be tougher. Examples are: Although an autohelm had been donated, Leslie thought having to steer the boat would keep the helmsman more alert. Actually, the autohelm would do a far better job; we wouldn't be as tired; and how can we watch for ice when our eyes are riveted to the compass needle? Carolann hit a piece of ice trying to steer by compass. The plumbing doesn't allow any toilet paper to go through, so all toilet paper is deposited in a plastic bag [which may be the reason toilet paper became a luxury item]. At one time water was pumped from the galley tap by means of a foot pedal. [David was mistaken about this—*Aqua Star*'s galley never had a foot pedal.] He replaced it with a hand pump. Now we have to wash one hand at a time, the idea being that less water would be consumed. Personally, I think it takes more. Another problem area is the anchor locker. The plastic pipe that the chain travels through is at only a slight angle and chain piles up in it. It takes

Two young fishermen provided the crew's dinner at Smokey Tickle: their only catch of the day, a salmon.

While the crew watched hungrily, one of the fishermen cut the salmon into thick steaks so that it could be easily cooked aboard Aqua Star.

three people—one at the helm, one at the chain locker, and one at the manual winch. So much simpler to have installed an electric winch with a switch at the helm. And our radar cannot be seen by the helmsman.

While Carolann and Gay took Leslie's word as law for the handling of the boat and navigation, David, though he was new to sailing, often decided that Leslie exaggerated the difficulties involved and grew to resent some of Leslie's autocratic ways. At the same time, David had the lightest load of responsibility for the success of the voyage, and he was the crew member least likely to understand Leslie's considerations and decision-making. After all, David had been the last person aboard on May 18, and he was never accountable for navigation or maintenance on board.

Cast off at 6:30 A.M. Another beautiful morning. But here closer to the coast is much colder. We pick our way through islands. Leslie is anxious because of rocks. (He should try the 30,000 Islands area of Georgian Bay!)

Leslie and Carolann are suffering from upset stomachs. Gay has complained for two days now. I believe it's the water. We all know it's bad and we do have some that is fresh, but I think Gay uses the bad water for cooking, tea, and coffee.

Gay did use the bad water for cooking, tea, and coffee, but with Leslie and Carolann's agreement, since they felt the cold temperatures in which they were sailing would protect them from bacteria. The controversy raged until the mysterious upsets all disappeared a few days later.

Leaving Hamilton Inlet, *Aqua Star*'s crew made more friends near a tiny cove misnamed on their chart, as Leslie explained.

That night the weather deteriorated to a full gale. At 3:30 A.M. we all jumped up, horrified—the anchor was dragging. By the time we managed to get on deck only half dressed and get the engine going, we were very close to a disaster. In the dark and driving rain, we picked up anchor, moved to another spot . . . it seemed okay . . . back to bed. By 7 A.M. the wind was up to 40 gusting to 50. Rain and fog. I started the engine and put it in gear to help take some strain off the anchor. Around 9 A.M. the wind slowed down and the rain stopped, but it was still foggy.

Later in the day we met two fishermen, Ed Whalen and Dexter Pierce from North Brigas, Newfoundland. They have come to the Labrador to fish for the past ten years. We invited them aboard and they gave us a 10-pound fish, their only catch of the day, and showed us how to fillet it. We offered them money for the fish, but they refused. Such is the hospitality of the people around here. We had a race to a small fishing community amongst the rocks called Smokey—the fishermen in their boat and us in our dinghy. There wasn't much to be found there except a grocery store, post office, and a dozen or so

houses—very isolated. Fuel was available, and at the fish plant
we picked up water, as we were preparing to leave the next day.
And leave we did at 5 A.M. Visibility was good—sunny and
almost warm. We will be heading towards Quaker Hat Island,
but from there we will be sailing very cautiously, as I haven't a
chart for an area of 50 miles or so to Makkovik.

Reading an unfamiliar coastline from seaward can be problematic
even with a chart. The difficulty now facing Leslie as he moved along
the coast was that the small settlements were unmarked; from the
deck of a boat, the distinguishing features that can be seen on a chart
merge—one piece of coast seems much like another. At the same
time, it was important to identify islands and other features correctly, or risk grounding the boat.

David took advantage of good weather to do some filming:

It's such a grand day I fell asleep sprawled on the aft deck. We
changed course and now the wind coming over the bow is cold.
We arrive at a cove near Smokey and anchor. I am dropped off
at a nearby shore and film Leslie and Carolann and several fishing boats (which stopped on their way in). We leave *Aqua Star*
for the community of Smokey. Good filming. Leslie and I fish
from shore and dinghy and catch two small cod, easily recognized by the small "finger" under the chin. We also catch and
throw back about 30 sculpin. We didn't know what they were,
such ugly but beautifully colored fish. Mostly head, they have
fins on the side that they fan out to make themselves look larger. They have large, brightly colored circles over them. I clean
and cook the cod for supper, clean up the kitchen, and hit the
sack, lulled to sleep by cold wind howling and moaning through
the rigging while *Aqua Star* rears on her anchor chain.

As *Aqua Star* came back out into the Atlantic, the sailing routine
changed. Ice and uncharted coastline made the daily passages north-
westward along the coast more demanding. Three days out of Goose
Bay, David reported that the crew was already tired:

None of us slept well. The boat was moving about all night in the high wind and the chain rumbling across the rock bottom kept each of us wondering if the next sound would be the anchor dragging. Tired bodies dragged themselves on deck at 6 A.M.

The day is somewhat chaotic. We experience dead calm and then six-foot swells. The sun is warm but it's mostly cloudy and cold. The thermometer reads 15°C (60°F) in the sun but we require our huge arctic boots and mitts. Sails up and down all day corresponding to weather and wind.

Then we see cells of rain about us and some moves over us. A belt of pack ice appears ahead. We are missing several charts for this area and find ourselves in the right church but wrong pew. I steer through the scattered field of ice with help from first Gay, then Carolann standing on the bowsprit and pointing out open areas.

The scenery is magnificent in its immense, tumbled rough-

Gay cut Carolann's hair while planes buzzed overhead in the busy harbor of Makkovik.

ness. We even see patches of black spruce amid the pockets of white snow on the ragged, purple hills. Toward evening we pull into a large inlet and revel in the quiet solitude and splendor. We haven't seen another boat all day. Mosquitoes are bad. Gay ventures out to smoke her cigarettes. We hit the sack under calm conditions about 10 P.M. Leslie and I, in the aft cabin, tell stories and laugh ourselves to sleep. The boat doesn't move all night, so we sleep soundly.

They arrived at the Labrador coastal settlement of Makkovik on a Thursday afternoon, and they planned to stay until 3 A.M. Saturday to satisfy Leslie's captainly superstition and everyone's need for a break. The harbor was abuzz with seaplanes, fishing boats, and helicopters as David filmed Gay cutting Carolann's hair in the cockpit. When they were allowed to take baths at the Grenfell Mission Hospital, they all learned a little Labrador history. The International Grenfell Association, whose mission is to care for the welfare of the Labrador people, was started some 75 years ago by Dr. Wilfred Grenfell. The association provides medical services and schools for the remote settlements, which, at the time it was established, were not in Canadian territory and had no central government capable of providing services. Carolann made a return trip to the hospital to take an *Aqua Star* brochure to an elderly fisherman who had heard about the expedition and was following the yacht's progress on a chart.

For sheer orneriness, Leslie met his match in Makkovik:

The highlight of our stay in Makkovik was when Dave and I met Aunt Susie—the rottenest person in all of Labrador. At least this is how everybody from Churchill to St. John's, Newfoundland, to Montreal referred to her, and I soon found out why. Susie won't let visitors to Makkovik have any booze. She has the only license to sell liquor in Makkovik and rules the town with an iron fist. Dave and I went to her and I said, "Could I buy a case of beer, please?" She looked at me with a cigarette butt hanging from her lips, holding a baby on her hip, and said, "Where ya from?" I said, "Toronto." She took the butt out of her mouth and with a loud yell she told me, "Ya should have brought your own goddam booze with ya. Now get out." I noticed when she yelled at me she only had two teeth in her whole head. I decided that I would put a curse on this woman for humiliating me like this, and the curse was that one of her two teeth should fall out and the remaining one should ache for the rest of her life.

The weather closed in on Saturday, preventing their departure. Cold, damp weather and waiting were relieved by Gay making one of her outstanding meals: caribou ribs, potatoes, and onions, followed by rhubarb pie. Even David commented, "Yum."

CHAPTER NINE

MAKKOVIK TO NAIN

From David's diary:

Sunday, July 28

U p at 3:30 A.M. Our bow riding light is shorted out. Once fixed, we up anchor. Foggy. We wend our way out to open water. Icebergs and bergy bits. Now the sea starts to build and the wind rises head-on. It's our worst weather yet. We all feel poorly. I must go forward to check the anchor. The bow dips into a wave and I'm up to my waist in water, my Arctic boots are filled. We are wet, cold, and miserable. And it gets worse. I try to film from the stern. Leslie and Gay raise the sails as I shoot 100 feet on the electric camera. Spray dashes over our heads and coats the camera lens. The boat pitches and tosses in the 10-foot swells and chop. When I go below to ready the camera, the motion soon has me ill and immobilized. It's only with tremendous effort that I can erect the tripod and mount the camera. Everything is sliding and bashing about. I nearly am tossed overboard several times as I try to keep the camera from dashing against the boom. Every chance I get I climb out of my wet gear and into my bunk for a quick nap, then back into the wet gear again for my watch. My socks and gloves are wrung out each time before I don them.

The alternator fails and we have to disconnect it. Then the Omega and radar quit for lack of battery power.

Almost suddenly in the late afternoon, the sun comes out and the seas become bearable. We anchor in Harrigan Island cove and fire up the generator to charge the batteries. We start to get things back in shape. The camera equipment is covered in salt spray. Leslie works on boat maintenance. The stuffing box is leaking again, and the girls start on supper. It's a beautiful, peaceful evening, but cold.

Next morning, Leslie recorded Crisis number 3. *Aqua Star* was trapped in pack ice:

At 5:30 A.M. I looked out and to my horror saw the whole anchorage filling up with pack ice. I yelled for everyone to get up immediately. Winched up the anchor, warmed the engine, and got the heck out of there. The ice was even worse farther out. Taking a chance on a lead, we motored for two miles, but it was closed by a big berg. Quickly I turned around. There were no more leads to try. The ice was getting worse. I thought, God, is this the end? Around 4 P.M. we were sitting in a hole about 200 feet in diameter in the ice, but slowly it, too, closed in. We didn't speak—everybody was looking in a different direction. Where there is ice there is fog, so you can't see very far. To break the silence, I asked Gay to make hot coffee. Then I spoke calmly to everybody: "We will try to get closer to shore or back to the anchorage. If we are going to be crushed by the ice, let's have it happen close to shore so we can get onto the land, unload some food and clothing, and if the end of *Aqua Star* comes, I'll activate the EPIRB and we'll wait for rescue."

Slowly pushing ice with the bow, we made it back to the anchorage. No need to drop the hook, as the ice was holding us secure. We went below. We didn't talk. Once in a while we heard the terrible sound of ice crunching against the side of the hull. Silently I took back the curse on Aunt Susie. Everyone was writ-

Gay wore a ski mask for warmth during the Labrador Coast passage. The weather was typically overcast with the July and August temperatures offshore hovering around 0° Celsius.

ing something. I wondered what the hell they were writing, but I wouldn't ask. The night went slowly. We didn't use any lights so as to save battery power. Some of the ice moved out during the night.

What the crew was writing was very different from Leslie's account. In her entry for the day, Gay concentrated on her personal life and the miserable state of her finances. David's story is so different that he and Leslie might have been on different boats:

I get up once in the night to put gas in the Honda generator. We are on course at 7 A.M. The water here is very clear. The Atlantic is peaceful now, with five-foot swells gently rocking *Aqua Star.*

PACK ICE, miles of it. The furnace was on all night and the girls' cabin is laced with lines, which are festooned with drying clothes. Gay burns the rice pudding and Leslie spills his coffee into the Omega, putting it out of commission. We are lost, so Leslie turns *Aqua Star* back to Harrigan Island to get his bear-

Aqua Star was twice trapped by pack ice—sparse at first, later surrounding the yacht, making any movement impossible. Each time, the crew was eventually able to pick a course through it, fending off smaller pieces.

ings. We start out again but the pack ice is too dense. We can't get through. Back to Harrigan Island, where we cruise in circles waiting and hoping a ship will come by so we can follow *it* through the ice to Nain. Gay burns the rice pudding again. It's thrown overboard. Gay puts the pot away dirty. I know her tricks. She will wait till I'm doing the dishes, then pull it out for me to clean. Ha.

9 P.M. I smell something burning and hear Leslie and Gay arguing. Les comes into the aft cabin and opens ports, mumbling about his boat being ruined. He is snoring a few minutes later. The girls call to me to come and see the sunset, complete with a rainbow. Les jumps up at 9:30 and has something to eat. I smell something burning again. I hear Les telling Gay, "Cooking isn't burning." And to just stay with the basics because getting fancy isn't working. About 10 P.M. Gay calls me for supper. I don't move.

Gay was certainly putting some wear and tear on Leslie's beautiful boat. By the time they reached Harrigan Island, she had put a hole in a counter shelf; sprayed Bug-Off on all the portlights, making them permanently hazy; put grease down the sink, so it was constantly plugged; spoiled a galley carpet; and set the oven on fire.

They began moving out of the encroaching ice late the next day, finding leads and slowly moving farther out to sea. For Leslie, it was a very close call:

That morning I tried to sound cheerful, but it was difficult. My whole life was in front of me. I have been in worse dangers before, but then I only had to look after myself. Trying to give a positive feeling to the group, I said, "Okay, guys, let's get serious—we have an expedition to finish." Engine going, slowly we pushed our way through the pack. As we moved into the open, there was so much ice we couldn't see the end of it. Motoring very slowly, we tried different leads in different directions. No luck. Again I asked Gay to make coffee. The mood of the group is now positive. Everybody talks like we used to—joking about what we are going to do after the expedition is over. David wants to go to McDonald's for a Big Mac; Gay is talking about the boat she is going to buy; Carolann is taking pictures and talking about our next cruise to Florida. I just listen and feel like praying, but not in front of everybody.

As I look over the charts at the navigation table, Gay hands me a coffee—Thanks! I turned the radio on at our designated time, wondering whether Polestar had been trying to locate us. Three days ago we had reported to them that we were fine. By now we should have been reporting to them from Nain. Then all of a sudden we hear...*Aqua Star, Aqua Star*...this is Rainbow Radio—over. Everyone stood around the radio as I reported to Polestar in Edmonton that *Aqua Star* has been trapped in pack ice for three days now, but there is no immediate danger to ship or crew. Then something very bad happened. When the radio came on, I had put my coffee on the chart table. As *Aqua Star* bounced off a piece of ice, the coffee tipped over, ran down the chart, and leaked into the Omega navigator. All the lights on the front went out and the digital numbers were wiped out—Crisis number 4.

God, what else—as if we don't have enough problems. Now we are without an alternator and without the Omega, and the Honda generator is low on gasoline. A sickening silence fell over the whole boat. I was mad. But at least we still had our Walker SatNav. A sextant here is useless. You only see the sun or the stars once a week. Now it is 5 P.M. and I am picking my way toward the south, where we came from. Short leads. Carolann noticed the fog had lifted a bit to the southeast, so she grabbed the binoculars and went up to the crow's nest. Five minutes later, she yelled like crazy that there was a long lead, and after that, loose ice only. I grabbed the binoculars and went up as fast as greased lightning. I looked...sure thing, there was a lead. I almost leaped from the crow's nest with happiness and told everyone to grab a boathook and be ready to fend off. I put her in gear and went for it.

We motored at five or six knots where we could see clear water and slowed down as the ice became thicker. By 8 P.M. we were on the other side of the pack ice and into the open Atlantic. Once again we are slowly motoring northward. With much happiness, we all hugged, kissed, and danced on deck yelling big yahoos. I quickly put the curse back on Aunt Susie. No way she was going to get off that easy.

This evening the temperature went down to -2°C. We had to stop motoring because we saw lots of ice again, but loose, so we just bobbed and took turns fending off the odd piece that would hit *Aqua Star.*

By midafternoon on July 31, *Aqua Star* was sailing the uncharted waters into Nain. They had reached the tree line—the point on their route above which trees of any size could no longer survive: the halfway point of the voyage. Gay was at the helm as they cautiously felt their way among the islands guarding the port. Notwithstanding a close call in suddenly shallowing waters, Leslie found a safe approach and all was well when they reached the town dock.

They spent 10 days in Nain. For the most part, it was an agonizing period of waiting for equipment to arrive before they could put out to sea again. Mel Woodward paid them a visit and arranged to have a new alternator flown in. David encountered every kind of hassle while trying to have two new camera bodies sent to him. For both parcels, the crew anxiously lingered, nervous about the Hudson Strait, impatient to complete the venture, eager to get on with the rest of their lives, and increasingly irritable with one another.

Carolann said that Nain reminded her of Muskoka, a resort area of Ontario. The town, although rough, has streetlights and signs reminding people to "Keep Nain Clean." It spreads at the foot of a mountain, and David commented as they approached that even from the harbor it seemed cleaner than many other settlements they had seen.

But Nain is also an uneasy mixture of Aboriginal and white people and ways of life, like so many northern communities. Unemployment and underemployment are prevalent, and in 1985, it was hard to find the pride and self-reliance more evident today among the aboriginal people of North America.

Many natives of Nain are people who were moved by the New-

The settlement of Nain, Labrador, the halfway point on Aqua Star's *voyage.*

A typical scene in Nain with Arctic cotton blowing in the breeze.

foundland government from more northern settlements, such as Hebron, because the government found it too expensive to send supplies to the scattered northern outports. As their fur trapping and fishing way of life became more tenuous because of the arrival of Europeans (trapping lines, for example, had to be longer and farther away from the summer bases, and fish stocks had been declining since the turn of the century), the settlements became dependent upon outside supplies and services. In 1959, the government cited the difficulty of transporting fuel, finding teachers, and providing medical services as their reasons for moving whole communities south to towns such as Goose Bay and Nain.

In Nain, a young Inuit woman asked if she could interview Leslie for the local radio station. She told him she was offended by the line in *Aqua Star*'s brochure that said the crew would record the native way of life, which had changed very little since the first explorers. They had to agree that she was right—life had changed in the north, and seldom for the better. Leslie's statements in the brochure, however, indicate that he did expect to find vital native settlements and make a record that would be a source of pride to his fellow Canadians. Instead, in some settlements—particularly those where the Cree and Inuit people were not self-governing—the conditions he found were far different from those in his more romantic vision.

Nain's shantytown is a place to be avoided at night, and violent incidents are common. In spite of Leslie's mission to document the way of life *Aqua Star* found in the small settlements on the coast, he and the others fell into the outsider's habit of playing tourist, meeting mostly other outsiders, like themselves, who could visit and leave at will. They met white northerners who passed on their own stories and opinions about native people. Some were prejudices and slurs— like the complaints they heard in Goose Bay about natives living in government-built houses and erecting tents inside them. Others were more well informed and reasoned. Native adults are often shy and seldom approach outsiders, so it's not surprising that much of what the *Aqua Star* crew learned about them was secondhand.

In Nain, Carolann made friends with two young Inuit girls, who carried her camera bags for her wherever she went. Carolann invited them for a visit to *Aqua Star,* a dinghy ride, and a tour of the boat, and she gave each a token of her friendship:

> I presented my little Inuit girlfriends with small gifts. Gwen (nine years) I gave a choice of either a blue bone-type necklace or a gold anchor with chain, as she was my favorite (very well mannered, intelligent, and sweet). She chose the anchor (her eyes grew twice their size and without hesitation she knew which one she wanted). Charlotte (eight years) was not around, so I told Gwen to make sure she received her gift. I also gave them the can of oranges they forgot to take with them from the boat. I hope they will write to me. When I have the photo of us together developed, I shall send them a copy.

The crew spent a lot of time with their fellow northern visitors— pilots, surveyors, and others. Many of the southerners they met in Nain and other settlements were employed by the governments— federal and provincial—to teach natives to work with new technologies in hospitals, schools, and radio and television stations. They were

Aqua Star's crew became tourists ashore, snapping sights like the Moravian Mission in Nain.

outsiders and usually highly paid—two factors that kept them very isolated from the natives.

The crew of *Aqua Star* was again offered the use of showers and laundries, and was made welcome in people's homes.

David enjoyed the hospitality immensely, but he was not always comfortable with the role of "*Aqua Star* crew member"—he was more interested in the places and people he met than in telling his own story. Carolann commented that he didn't give anything of himself to the people they met. But David the introvert also found it easy to make friends in port because of the expedition's high profile:

We dinghy to shore and meet "the fellas" over breakfast. One of the new faces is a young helicopter pilot, Norman, who will take me up for pictures of *Aqua Star*. We wash our clothes in the hotel. Norman and I have a great conversation about flying. He takes the rear door off the chopper and I strap up a seat belt that will allow me to lean out with one foot on the skid. I have two 35mm cameras and the movie camera. Norm gives me two more 35s. *Aqua Star* is sailing beautifully when we come over her. I click away, feverishly changing camera after camera. The movie camera is jumping all over in the wind and jerky movements of the chopper. I can't steady against the framework. It's too jumpy. I try shooting at 64 fps, but I am not satisfied. Even the still shots are too hurried, and he peels off before I am through. I'm sure the results will be disappointing. I think fixed-wing aircraft are far easier to shoot from. I got to handle the helicopter.

We visit with a group of three people: Keith, Carol, and Lynn, who are kayaking along the Labrador coast for two weeks, and we spend a pleasant two hours—except I think our group from *Aqua Star* (a) talks too much and (b) talks too much about all the things we've done. I think we wear out our welcome.

Leslie wanted to check the propeller shaft and decided to move *Aqua Star* as close to shore as possible and let her rest on her keel when the tide went out, working quickly to finish before the tide returned. Since Nain's dock was the town meeting place, he provided the day's entertainment for a social gathering on the pier.

Gay took advantage of every opportunity to get off the boat. In Nain she met young men her own age who were happy to have company. For the others, it was a relief that she was off the boat. Sometimes she seemed to try to toe the line, while other times she seemed to be testing the limits.

Woke at 7:30 A.M., having had only one hour of sleep. Back to boat with dinghy by 9 A.M. Carolann angry, Leslie angry— shit. I guess I just don't realize others' sense of discipline. They make me feel like an unruly monster, and all I meant was to enjoy myself—NOT to upset others. If they only knew how much I hate being in shit—felt dreadful. Met Norm today. He generously offered to fly David to film *Aqua Star* sailing in the bay! Sunny and windy: Carolann, Leslie, and I feeling lucky as the helicopter cruised around the sails. The sailwork was uplifting and revitalizing. The ugliness of the morning dissipated. David and Norm joined us on *Aqua Star* for coffee, then all went ashore to Norm's room for beer (only guests at the hotel can buy). [This is a curious arrangement common in the north. In the hotels (often trailers strung together), hotel guests are allowed to buy beer, while natives, who seldom stay in the hotels as guests, can buy only hard liquor outside. It's a practice designed to prevent or discourage drinking, but in effect it forces natives to stick to hard liquor.]

Conversation with Norman was lively—he's been everywhere. He had a conversation with Carolann regarding the natives and the system that supports their sad lifestyle.

Carolann and the rest seemed distant, so I stayed on Norm's invite.

But Gay seldom followed through with her good intentions, as a note in David's journal attests:

Late tonight, Gay burns hole in mainsail with cigarette. Les blasts her. We talk about leaving her behind.

At this point in the passage, the problem of shoestring finances began to add to the friction. Gay was down to a few borrowed dollars. Carolann and Leslie were tightening the reins on the little money they had left. Carolann took inventory and announced that everyone would have to buy their own "goodies." Gay reported her reaction to the situation:

Carolann did a little shopping and cannot afford toilet paper, etc. I've been off boat, thank God—I'd rather starve than hear the nitpicking counting and rationing that must go on. Oh dear, oh my. Making matters worse that I cannot access my own cash in Toronto. We may be here for a week! David lent me $20 to be paid back in Churchill. Thank you, David!

The friends they made among the staff of the Grenfell Mission Hospital had given them a care package: tins of milk, Kool-Aid, home-baked cookies and cake, and a chicken. David could still afford to share the wealth, but he also shared in the privations Leslie decreed for the rest of the trip:

Making friends in Nain—a chance to meet Inuit and others and enjoy their interest in the voyage.

We discuss the fact that (1) there will be only a small quantity of fuel for the furnace, enough for only a few hours on the very coldest days; (2) there is no money left and we are nearly out of toilet paper; (3) we can only carry 10 liters of kerosene for the stove and when that's gone, we will eat any food uncooked with no coffee or tea; (4) we will have to covet our water supply and govern its use very carefully.

We are quite a tough crew now, used to discomfort, terribly irregular hours, hard work, and being cold, tired, wet, and hungry. I notice that I slip naked into an ice-cold sleeping bag without whimpering any more and open the portlight above my head even though we are without heat and the outside temperature is 4°C.

On August 7, David and Leslie went fishing. A few days earlier, David had caught his first Arctic char; now it was Leslie's turn:

The wind is now in the east and the weather has turned raw. Les and I put on our foulweather suits, jump in the dinghy, and head for a shoreline about seven km away. It appears much closer, everything does. The dinghy is a superb piece of equipment

The nurses of Nain added to Aqua Star's *dwindling provisions with a package containing cookies, cake and chicken.*

and survives some punishment. The drawback to using it is the arduous task of lifting its motor off its bracket on the stern of *Aqua Star,* carrying its lumpy 60 lbs. along a narrow deck strewn with lines, and then lowering it to the gallant lad standing in the dinghy. He says an act of contrition, takes a deep breath, and then goes into a routine of quaking legs and quivering torso. It's really a dangerous situation, for if your feet move to port, the dinghy moves an equal distance to starboard. It's very similar to standing on a tightrope. If any kind of sea is running, the tightrope is being violently shaken. So far the only damage has been bumps and bruises.

Bouncing through and over the waves at full throttle is invigorating. And teeth-rattling. We tie up along the boulder-strewn shore and stand in awe at the meadow of white-plumed Arctic cotton nodding in the breeze against a background of red fireweed. Black spruce dot slopes that rise to jagged peaks.

We cast from shore, and Arctic char rise to the red-and-white spoon. The rod bends as the line stretches away, cutting the sun's face with zigzags. The char is a beautiful fish. Very slim and streamlined, with a small head. Its silver sides are topped by a back of gray-green. I catch three, each weighing about four pounds, and several slightly smaller, which I release. They are a thrill to handle. Leslie catches two, his first char, and now knows why I was so excited about them. We've been here about half an hour. The fishing's good, mosquitoes bad, so we bounce our way back to *Aqua Star,* where I clean the catch. We enjoy a soup made from some of the fish, and the rest are cut into sections and fried. We eat this till we just can't down any more, then we sit back to the sound of Percy Faith and speak with reverence of the flavor of this red-fleshed species. The beauty of this area and the fishing experience will stay with me a long time. I do the cleaning up. Then bed.

Finally, David's parcel arrived on August 10 and *Aqua Star* left Nain, heading for Saglek, 150 nautical miles to the north. As they left port, they wrote in their journals that they hoped to see their new acquaintances again.

After days of hearing Leslie vent his frustration at having to linger in port, everyone was pleased to get underway.

As Gay said, it never ends, and the arguments continued unabated. But now the end of the trip was in sight and there was a very strong feeling that they should pull together and finish what they had started. For all the friction, things weren't so very bad, as Gay told me before she left Nain.

> Spoke to Judy Chopra from Nain. She's worried about us. Doesn't want us to whitewash things. Well...we won't, but it'll be hard for non-*Aqua Star* members to understand it all. Between food disputes, tempers, conditions outside our control, it's bloody amazing that things are half as good as they are. Though I must admit I've enjoyed being nine days in Nain by myself. Leslie simply asked me to be back on Friday morning to clean *Aqua Star* before departure. No problem, that's fair.

Aqua Star *under sail.*

Chapter Ten

✦

Nain to Hudson Strait

Sailing now became uppermost on everyone's mind. Several times during the next few days, they decided to sail all night, to keep going while the weather was with them. The mid-September deadline for crossing Hudson Bay was looming closer. David reported good sailing on August 12:

> We were anchored on rock and held our breaths all night, listening to the scraping sounds of the chain and pig shifting about. And so our sleep was fitful. When we arose at 4 A.M., *Aqua Star* hadn't moved. We headed out to sea, past the towering Torngat Mountains that embrace the fjord.
>
> We've had to change our heading to 040° to allow for drift, as the SatNav shows our position each time as closer and closer to land.
>
> It's a beautiful day. Although seas appear calm, *Aqua Star* never ceases to pitch and roll to some degree in the swell. The scenery is spectacular, with peaks and huge icebergs. The girls pose with a huge iceberg in the background—Carolann in her Tilley shorts, and Gay flashing (expose yourself to an iceberg) as though for a poster.

The brooding Torngat Mountains line the northern tip of the Labrador Coast.

Just as I put the camera down, a large chunk of ice crashes into the sea. Leslie brings up the rifle, but three shots fail to cause more to fall while the camera rolls.

I had a nice nap sprawled on the dinghy.

It's 7°C. We have sunshine out here 20 miles from the coast, but black clouds heave and tumble all along through the mountains. The rainstorms are spectacular.

Les is very cheerful because we are closing in on Cape Chidley and the Hudson Strait. We will go all night. It's very good sailing right now and we are making six knots.

Tonight we had chicken soup. Delicious. Last night Gay cooked legs and breasts—also delicious. Crew is in good spirits.

It's a lovely evening. A beautiful sunset lays a pink mist over the coastal mountains. We comment on the grotesque shapes of the hills and the wild array of cloud formations. Later, we crane our necks to watch the soft veils of green Northern Lights shift and twine around. We have to regularly change course 5° as currents drift us toward shore.

Leslie had planned to rest at Port Burwell before crossing Ungava Bay:

Daylight came early. By 4:30 we could see Cape Chidley and the Gray Strait. Just to the north was Button Island at the entrance of Hudson Strait. Oh, WOW! Everybody is up. The safest way is to go north of Button Island, then turn south to Port Burwell. We decided to take a chance and go through Gray Strait. We entered the strait and within an hour it was dark again. The weather got very nasty. Strong wind was funneling through the strait. Fog rolled in from the hills and the rain poured until we could hardly open our eyes. Damn it! We should have gone the other way. According to the Sailing Directions, Port Burwell was an abandoned Moravian mission. I only wanted to anchor and rest before we cross Ungava Bay, but now I just want to get there. Close to the entrance of Port Burwell, there was so much pack ice we didn't think it possible to get inside . . . but slowly we pushed ahead. As we got farther in, we looked ahead and through the fog saw a ship . . . could we be this tired? Or is it a ship? As we continued, we saw a Coast

The Coast Guard provided Leslie with the latest weather and ice reports before he entered the Hudson Strait.

A helicopter airlifted construction materials for a new radio base from the Norman McLeod Rogers.

Aqua Star *safely rafted alongside the* Norman McLeod Rogers *while her crew enjoyed the Coast Guard captain's hospitality.*

Guard icebreaker, *Bernier.* Soon a helicopter overhead, then another helicopter. I heard a call on the VHF...it was coming from a second icebreaker in the inner harbor, *Norman McLeod Rogers.* The captain told us to continue in and tie up on their starboard side. Yes, sir! Thank you. The crew of *Aqua Star* was jumping up and down on deck. Boy, half an hour ago they were almost dying and now look at them! As we approached the icebreakers, we could see a lot of people waiting with cameras as soon as *Aqua Star* emerged from the fog. They were taking pictures of us. We tied up alongside the *Norman McLeod Rogers.* God, what a feeling.

Then a man leaned over the rail and yelled to us: "The captain would like to see all of you aboard his ship." After meeting Captain Gerard Guesneau, a fine gentleman, he (here we go again) invited us for dinner that evening. But first we all had a beautiful shower, put on clean clothes—the girls even put on makeup and some perfume—we looked civilized. We arrived at the captain's cabin, where he offered us Dubonnet on ice and told us how much he appreciated what we were doing and how much he admired us all. Then a call came on the public address system for us to go to the dining room. Here again, white tablecloth, two vases, each with a red rose, and a waiter with a menu who took our orders. After dinner, we returned to the captain's cabin where we were served cognac and had more interesting conversation. We thanked the captain for the lovely evening and went back to *Aqua Star,* started the heater, and talked for a while about how lucky we are to find such hospitality even in a ghost town.

They hadn't been in Port Burwell long before there was more of the infighting that they all loathed but all contributed to. Once again, Gay had found a berth off *Aqua Star,* and somehow she got into Leslie's line of fire. But as David explained, it didn't dampen their spirits as they began their crossing of Ungava Bay:

I don't know what happened after I went to sleep last night. But when I woke at 7 A.M., Leslie's bed was still made, so I thought he'd spent the night with Carolann in the front cabin, which meant that Gay stayed aboard the ship again. And I thought we were leaving at 3 A.M.

I lay in my bunk and wrote a letter to Anna, waiting for someone to move. Finally, at 8:30 I heard Leslie and Carolann. Breakfast (coffee and Arctic char). It was given to us by the fishing boat that pulled up alongside yesterday. The fish had been cooked (fried) last night, but no one was hungry.

Les and Carolann are angry with Gay, blaming her for our late departure. But Leslie told me he had been partying till 3:30 this morning. Neither would go for Gay, so I did. The captain came with Gay to *Aqua Star*. He's a real gentleman. He brought a bottle of wine. Carolann is nasty to Gay and of course there is no need for it. It only creates more tension and ill-feeling, the very things she accuses Leslie of.

I I A.M.: It's a dull, cold morning, about 2°C, as we give and receive three horn blasts from the *Rogers*. They had all been very friendly and helpful. Marcel, a helicopter pilot who had come aboard *Aqua Star* only half an hour ago, flew alongside us now and gave us a thumbs-up. Then he flew ahead, turned, roared past, and veered up in a spectacular climb. What a great feeling we have. We also now get reciprocal three blasts from the *Bernier* and waves from all. We set our course at 320° and head across calm waters toward Cape Hopes Advance, 160 miles away on the far side of Ungava Bay.

Ice. Les gets up in the crow's nest and yells down to me and points. I steer 025° and we skirt around it and resume 320°. Another ice edge—or "oice age," as the Newfoundland weather reports say. (At first we thought they were talking about how old the ice was.) Row after row. And bits that we zigzag through. We spot a seal on an ice floe, head our bow toward it, and cut the engine revs. As we get closer, it rears up, peering at this strange thing. I set the camera at 64 fps and shoot off short bursts. The sea is quite calm, but *Aqua Star* still bounces and I can't get a stable platform for my camera on the pulpit and still see the seal, which is lower than our railing. I do get a nice shot of it as it humps toward the edge and dives over with a splash. All shot at 64 fps and camera on auto. Crew all getting along at the moment. Gay is especially high, feeling relief at not getting a blast from Leslie. Leslie has headache from party and gets aspirin.

French onion soup (complete with cheese on bread) for lunch. Yum.

Les and I are on watch from nine till midnight. At 12, as we prepare to end our shift, our searchlight picks up chunks of ice. I am shining the light back and forth ahead, while Leslie steers through. I work till 1 A.M. with the light while the girls take down the sails.

I go to my bunk. It's very cold in the aft cabin.

Encountering ice in the darkness or being caught in pack ice during a storm were among the perils Leslie had envisioned on the Labrador Coast. For Carolann, being surrounded by ice in the black of night was one of the most frightening events of the voyage.

Leslie consistently requested the best information he could get on weather, sailing conditions, and ice from the professionals he encoun-

A small visitor rests aboard Aqua Star.

tered along the way. Armed with ice reports and forecasts from the Coast Guard, he was ready to cross Ungava Bay with some confidence.

Ungava Bay is scooped out of the Hudson Strait southwest of Cape Chidley, the northernmost point of Labrador. From here until Hudson Bay, *Aqua Star* would be in Quebec territory. Most important for the crew, Ungava Bay was 160 nautical miles of open-water sailing. This was the kind of sailing Leslie had imagined when he planned the expedition, and he tackled it with some bravado and his customary caution:

At 11 A.M. I received the updated weather on VHF. Looked good—wind light to moderate from the northeast. At noon we were riding the ice edge. We then proceeded to enter into the loose pack from the north-northwest. After about eight miles of maneuvering, we could see the lead was not exactly clear, but good enough. Another five miles and we should be on the other side of the pack. I reported our good fortune to the *Norman McLeod Rogers*. The radio operator had my time schedule for calling Edmonton and said, "I will listen on your frequency and if you can't get through, I will try to boost your message to Edmonton and to *Neddrill II*." Thank you, Jacques.

At 6 P.M. we were motorsailing in a light northeast wind—quite cold. At approximately 9 P.M., I stared in disbelief. Are my eyes deceiving me? God, this wasn't on the ice chart. It looks like ice ahead, but as we get closer, we see it is fairly loose. Picking a lead, we drop sails and continue under power, zigzagging between the pack. After 10 miles of tense maneuvering, it seemed we were in the open again. The cold is draining our energy, making us tense and miserable. We put on extra clothing. I try VHF, but we're out of range now. The crew puts sails up again while I go down to check SatNav and mark the spot where we met this pack ice. The Omega navigator never recovered from the coffee bath. We now have to navigate by SatNav alone, because we are about 800 miles from the magnetic pole, making the magnetic compass unreliable.

11 P.M. Carolann calls me to the radar to look. No! I can't take any more of this. Looks like ice four miles ahead. We take up

our positions on deck, boathooks and spotlights ready. There are small pieces of ice, and as we get closer, we can see a white line in front of us. I take the wheel. Sails are brought down. David positions himself at the bow with a powerful spotlight, Gay and Carolann on either side with boathooks. The radar screen is cluttered . . . nothing but ice after two hours of pushing and shoving—we can't see any lead. I make a vow never to enter ice again at night. As we proceed, I make a great many more promises. The barometer is going down. God! If a storm blows up, we are finished if we don't get out of this ice. Again, everyone is very quiet. Only the haunting sound of ice and its movement in the pack. I take the curse off Aunt Susie . . . my whole life is in front of me again.

Time goes very slowly. Please, morning, come so I can see. Every once in a while, a big piece of ice pushes *Aqua Star* completely out of the way. The sickening sound on the hull is enough to make one very religious. This goes on all night until finally at 6 A.M. there is enough light to see. From the crow's nest I pick up a lead and we head toward it. After half an hour, I'm up the mast to look for another lead. Up and down, up and down, like a yoyo, when finally it looks like it is loosening up ahead. Our spirits lift just to think we are going out into clear water again. Another hour and we are almost in the clear. Just some big bergy bits around us now.

On one of the ice floes we see a big harp seal and go toward him with cameras ready. We take his picture before he slips into the icy waters. What a relief to once again be heading in the right direction. There is less and less ice, so we decide to put up sails again. On the horizon we spot a ship. I check on the radar—she is heading east. I tried to contact her on VHF and was successful after two tries. A female voice reported that the *Viking* had just come through the Hudson Strait. I asked if there was any ice. She said, "No ice at all—not even a small piece." I told them they were heading right into pack ice. "I know—we were in it all night." They thanked me and I wished them good luck. Then, I turned to my crew and said, "Did you guys hear that? No more ice. Yahoo!"

I put the curse back on Aunt Susie, asked Gay to make fresh coffee, then checked our position. We should be in Diana Bay, Koartac Harbor, this afternoon. We made contact with *Neddrill II* for the first time. Yahoo again. Jacques, from *Norman McLeod Rogers,* cut in. He told us the weather looked good for at least the next two days. By two in the afternoon, we enter the harbor and drop the hook. We are exhausted but happy, and we congratulate each other after making our first crossing of a large body of water.

The crew anchored and went ashore to the small village of Koartac, the most traditional Inuit settlement they had yet encountered. That afternoon and the next day, they met many of the local people, some of whom visited *Aqua Star* in their own boats. Leslie enjoyed these visits: They reinforced his notion that the expedition was breaking new ground.

In the early morning a lot of native people—fishermen, stone carvers, seal and caribou hunters—visited *Aqua Star.* They came out with long, open wooden boats, some with 70 hp motors. They just rammed *Aqua Star* to come to a full stop. Everyone would stand up, hang onto the gunwale of *Aqua Star* to hold themselves steady, and just silently look. I came on deck to shake hands with everyone. If there is one among them who can speak English, the first thing he'll ask (the women never speak) is, "How fast can this boat go?" These people have never seen a sailboat before. When we made the claim to become the first sailboat to cross the Hudson Bay, we did four years' research to be sure. We contacted Carl Vilas, the historian of the Cruising Club of America. After a lot of searching, we found a book, *North to Baffin Island,* by John T. Rowland, which is the story of three young men who set out to deliver a 30-foot yawl, *Darryl,* to a Hudson Bay post in the Arctic in 1910. They made it as far as Erik Cove on the Hudson Strait . . . but I doubt if any of these native people were alive then.

Early that evening, I plotted our next course and decided to leave Koartac just after midnight in order to arrive at Wakeham Bay in daylight. Anchor up and underway by 0100. Very dark night, no moonlight, wind on the nose and motoring—cold, 0°C. I went to sleep for an hour. The crew didn't wake me. They decided everything was fine. Gay took over and they allowed me to get some extra sleep...thanks, guys!

Once again they sailed beyond their destination, bypassing Wakeham Bay and continuing on to Deception Bay. In the dark early hours of the morning, while Gay and Carolann were on watch, they saw a dense red light in the distance. Their first thought was that it was a ship. Then it became larger and changed shape—it looked like the flame of a candle. They deliberated and finally decided to wake Leslie. All three watched and waited on deck, eventually realizing that what they were watching was an Arctic sunrise.

Gay made some candid remarks about her feelings on this passage. True for the moment, they show how impatient everyone was to be finished:

> Depart Koartac 1 A.M. for Wakeham Harbor. . . . I love reading the charts. I'm so anxious to get to the *Neddrill II* oil rig and then on to Churchill—success and back to being independent. Yeah! Can't wait to see Matt—hope I can lose eight pounds fast. . . . I want to be skinny! Hope Leslie doesn't hang around too much in bays and settlements. I'm losing enthusiasm for the historical, cultural aspect—ONLY CARE ABOUT SAILING *Aqua Star* TO CHURCHILL.
>
> I help Les by doing his log in evening and naviplotting. Hudson Strait like glass! Heading for Deception Bay, where we hope to find *Sir John Franklin* icebreaker for fuel. Will skip Wakeham Bay.

David, too, was anxious to complete the trip. He was still calmer and less inclined to be carried away with the drama of the voyage than the others:

We motored all night in dead calm. Very uneventful. Leslie frets about islands, shoals, etc. The radar confirms our location along with the SatNav, but Leslie hasn't any experience yet and so doesn't trust anything, nor does he delegate. Gay or myself could do the navigating while he sleeps. He really exaggerates the dangers. Anyone could do the navigating we are doing. I'm embarrassed when he talks to these people about his work on *Aqua Star* because they do it all the time under very tough conditions at times and think nothing of it.

In Deception Bay, the crew of *Aqua Star* encountered a herd of caribou. David climbed to the top of a cliff to photograph *Aqua Star* riding at anchor below. Carolann caught her first Arctic char—the largest of the expedition:

The quest for Arctic char occupied Leslie's precious leisure time at anchor.

Relaxing in a meadow at Deception Bay, Gay discovered it was a sea of blueberries.

I took up David's fishing rod (he was on top of the cliff taking pictures of *Aqua Star* moored in the bay). I had no sooner thrown it in than a five-pound Arctic char caught onto the hook. It was beautiful to see this great fighter trying to outsmart me (which it almost did). This was a very exciting moment, and with the help of Gay we managed to get the fish on shore. Gay collected mussels and that night we had a feast. Gay and David also had a great time picking blueberries as I sat on a boulder reminiscing and becoming quite overtaken by the serenity of this place. I saw something huge jump into the water but never did discover what it was.

We saw eight caribou come down through the tidal flat to the water's edge (tide was out). They were about to swim across but caught our scent and retreated back and up through the valley—it was wondrous to see how they all relied on the head of the herd before making their move.

> *Overleaf: A herd of caribou was the highlight of the crew's stop in Deception Bay, the most beautiful anchorage of the voyage.*

Deception Bay was a magical anchorage, a refreshing pause in a voyage that had lost its focus.

Aqua Star's crew left Deception Bay with new commitment to completing the expedition.

Five canoes laden with tricycles, women, children, and caribou hunters came alongside *Aqua Star.* We welcomed them and
had a great talk telling them our good fortune of seeing the caribou, which they were sorry to have missed. They put up camp
on shore and were gone very early the following morning to
better hunting grounds. One of the young boys gave David a
seashell for a gift.

Carolann described her response to the barren shores of the bay as
a religious experience. These few quiet anchorages and long passages
away from the pressures of other people reminded the crew of their
reasons for being there—often hard to focus on in port. And the still-
ness they found restored some of their own personal equilibrium—
the majesty of nature demanded their attention, so the cacophony
below decks took a distant back seat for a time. In port, the team spirit tended to break apart as soon as *Aqua Star* docked—everyone want-

ed a chance to be alone. David and Gay wanted to be individuals instead of members of "the crew of *Aqua Star*." On this final leg of the trip, each member of the group was committed to the teamwork required to complete the job, but the time spent in settlements was perceived as time wasted.

Nevertheless, *Aqua Star* spent four days in port at Salluit, the crew's last harbor before Hudson Bay. Once again they made some local friends and stocked up on fuel and fresh food. Nora Ikey, the town radio operator, met Leslie and Carolann as they walked down its main street. She invited them for coffee and offered the help of her son, the police chief, in filling *Aqua Star*'s fuel and water tanks. Earlier, in Koartac, they had met Mike Keelan, who had invited them to use his home for showers and filming interviews. Mike had given them some hard-to-come-by oranges when they left. They were also guests of the mayor of Koartac, who invited them into her home. Now, in Salluit, they met people who provided them with fresh bread and offered to lend them cash to tide them over to Churchill. And, as in every port, the crew never wanted for showers or access to telephones.

But among the crew themselves, the breaking point was coming. Even David's reserve was weakened. Here are some of his entries for the days they spent in Salluit.

Nora Ikey gave us a caribou roast, but when the oven is turned on, it bursts into flames. It hasn't been turned off properly and kerosene has leaked into it. Poor Les is distraught at his $1,000 stove and the smoke. All the vents are open. My clothes smell of kerosene. It's cold, and I'm tired.

Les asks me to take over the galley and cooking. And to cook the roast NOW. So in it goes at 350°F. It's 10 P.M.

I light the Coleman in the aft cabin for a little comfort.

Carolann comes aboard and takes over the roast. She says it's done; Leslie says it needs another hour. I go to sleep but wake up and smell it burning. I think I'll stay out of it.

We get up and go out to the galley. The roast is a cinder. Leslie says, "At least it's sterilized." Ha. I chop the meat from the bone. Leslie holds out his hand for the bone. I ask if

he's going to chew on it. "Do you want me to growl, too?" he asks.

Leslie has never (1) cleaned our head; (2) washed a dish; (3) prepared a meal; (4) said please or thank you to the girls; (5) praised the girls for anything they have done. He told me on several occasions and again last night that women are absolutely useless and will ruin everything they come near. And he is absolutely serious.

Up, breakfast, dishes, and raise anchor. Leslie can't manage to get his soft-boiled egg out of the shell and is exasperated. He complains about skim milk on cereal and I butter bread because he puts it on in huge chunks. I have to explain that we are into our last carton.

I use 25mm lens to film our departure from foggy Digges Islands. Gay complains when I ask to repeat a sequence for the camera and I tell her off. Crew are surprised at my first show of temper, but I am tired of their redundant chatter—telling me

Power for the town of Salluit on the Hudson Strait is supplied by a diesel generator. Fuel ships anchor offshore and pipes carry the town's diesel to onshore storage tanks.

Aqua Star's crew had help taking on fuel and making final preparations for Hudson Bay while spending four days in Salluit. The town's constable and his wife collected fuel containers and transported them in their outboard to Aqua Star, *anchored offshore.*

things I knew 30 years ago. I feel like telling them all off, but will try to keep peace for the two weeks remaining.

Water rough as we leave shelter of cove. My hands are freezing from exposure and pulling weeds off anchor. Operating camera almost impossible. Yet my body is overheated and soaked with sweat from effort.

Water washing over me and camera as I try to get good footage. This saltwater soaking is bad for camera, but I feel essential for film. Magazine 65 has mainsail going over to other side as girls work the winches.

Writing terrible because of cold and very rough seas.

After my watch from 2 to 3 a.m. I go to the aft cabin and change all my clothes. I'm now more comfortable, as my others were wet. I'm glad I brought enough warm, dry clothes on this trip. I have several more dry changes if I need them.

We go around Mansel Island and head into Hudson Bay.

I try to dry some camera equipment. Most got saturated with

salt water as I worked with it. It's extremely difficult to work as I am catapulted violently about and must sacrifice myself as I try to protect my equipment from being smashed.

Clouds clear away at sundown as we pass Mansel Island on our port side. It's the last land we will see on the way to the Canterra drill ship *Neddrill II,* for we are now crossing Hudson Bay.

We will maintain one-hour watches tonight. Leslie says he has too much to do, especially checking our course, so he won't go to sleep tonight.

He could sleep all night, getting up hourly for 10 minutes to do all that is necessary. Even that isn't called for, as it's open water with no hazards. Later, Leslie does just that.

The sea becomes quite placid and when on watch we enjoy the Northern Lights.

CHAPTER ELEVEN

❀

HUDSON BAY

By Monday, August 26, *Aqua Star* was crossing Hudson Bay in heavy weather that was to last several days.

The last entry in Carolann's diary was for Deception Bay. After that evening of peace and attention—Gay wrote, "Carolann, you're a star!" because she had caught the largest Arctic char of the voyage—Carolann was just holding herself together, waiting for the misery to end:

> Crossing the Hudson Strait, I experienced something strange. The wind had come up and it was my watch. It was dark—the water was black and eerie. I heard a noise and then I thought that one of the crew was calling me. Then I heard a voice—I thought it was my mother and I spoke to her and then I just listened. When I came off my watch and went below, I continued to hear the voice. Gay said that she had heard voices too.

Carolann now, as the weather worsened, had to deal with the misery of extreme seasickness as well as the emotional pain the voyage had caused her. She compounded the problem by taking her usual four Gravol tablets plus two Transderm patches that Gay applied later in a kind of kill-or-cure attempt to get Carolann back on her feet.

I had taken four Gravol pills just prior to the storm coming into full force, but still got seasick. I was afraid to go below, but I was freezing (mostly from the fact I was sick). Gay got me to come below and took off my clothes for me—bless her. I was sick immediately. I ran to the head and that is where I remained for three days. It was constant—no letup. Climb, climb, and then slam—*Aqua Star* seemed to twist with the impact.

With the Transderm overdose, Carolann finally had relief from nausea, although she was still incapacitated: She couldn't focus her eyes or speak clearly. For the duration of the storm, *Aqua Star* effectively had a crew of three.

Four times as large as all the Great Lakes together, Hudson Bay demanded all of the skills and endurance that Leslie, Gay, and David had developed since leaving Toronto. If the sailing and navigation had so far been untroubled, it was now a real test of their strength, both mental and physical.

Watches were extremely dangerous, requiring safety harnesses to hold them to *Aqua Star*'s rigging as they moved about on the treacherous decks. Staying on course required both accurate navigation by Leslie and attention to the helm by the crew as *Aqua Star* tossed in the heavy seas.

Sailing in 30-foot waves, Carolann says, is like going up in an elevator—then the cable breaks and you slam back down again. Add to this snow and ice-cold water washing over the crew, through their foulweather gear and into their Arctic boots. And there was no respite for days: The torment was broken only by incidents of extraordinary danger struggling to stay aboard the bucking yacht.

At one point while I was below, I heard Gay shouting from the helm. Although I'd taken off my gear, I rushed up. She pointed forward and shouted, "Help Leslie!" At first, when I saw him lying on the deck, I thought he was hurt, but as I rushed forward I saw he was attempting to bring down the jib, but the powerful wind was blowing it up. I leapt onto Leslie's back and then crawled forward over him and gathered in armfuls of sail. Eventually it was tied down.

David was twice airborne when coming on deck before he had a chance to attach his safety line. The crew took one-hour watches, with two hours off, and while off-watch lay wedged in the companionway below. There was no point in changing into dry gear because it would be drenched as soon as they went on deck. At one point, Gay risked standing on deck to shout at God.

On August 27, David reported that *Aqua Star* was hove-to for the night—a maneuver Leslie had never before attempted, but one that is called for when a vessel can make no headway and the crew is exhausted. With *Aqua Star*'s rudder bound in one direction and a reefed main bound in the opposite direction, she essentially stalled, and although she continued to drift, she was no longer being blown off course, so her crew could rest.

There is some abatement today, but it continues cold, rainy, windy, and very loppy. Carolann is still out of it and feeling badly at not being able to keep her watch. Gay is angry when Les tells her about tardiness when relieving on watch. She argues, What's a few minutes? but NEVER has she been a few minutes early. And it's five minutes to 20 minutes. She has taken some medicine for seasickness that causes her to throw up. But she can still function. It's noon hour.

Leslie is feeling ill as well and puts the chimney in place and lights the fire. Our wet clothes are everywhere. We are too tired to eat. I'm sore all over from the effects of sailing under these conditions. We are going nowhere, so we all go below and the engine is shut off. *Aqua Star* drifts quite well as we try to sleep at 1 P.M.

It's now 9:30 in the evening. We continue to drift, and will do it all night.

I went out at 8 P.M. to shoot film. It's very rough, with 30-foot waves. My safety harness keeps me on board as *Aqua Star* lurches and heaves.

Inside, *Aqua Star* is in chaos. Gear, mostly dry now, is strewn about. If it's hung up, the next wave hurls it across the cabin.

Leslie can't sleep in his bunk, as he is rolled constantly, so he sleeps on the floor in the narrow passageway. I will stay with my bunk, as floor is wet from salt water off our raingear.

Gay has made us orange drink and sandwiches of ham and sliced onion. Yum. Just now I was again hurled into the far bulkhead. The sandwich is our first and only meal today. Gay eats more.

It's a wonder one of us hasn't sustained a serious injury under these rough conditions. The boat is constantly rolling and heaving. But every few minutes she is hit solidly by a big superwave that causes her to twist violently, and we hear and feel the crash of the water sweeping over us.

We are drifting in a southeasterly direction, which is okay, as the rig is south of us. We have drifted about 10 miles.

I cannot sleep, but lie in my bunk and hang on as the rough seas toss *Aqua Star* about.

Filmed no one on helm.

Leslie said being in the storm was like being in a small car inside a cement mixer. Radio contact with *Neddrill II* indicated first that the weather was due to improve by midday on the 28th, then on the 29th, and finally it did improve on the 30th. The frustration at being hove-to and making no progress toward their destination began to make the crew tense. At one point, Leslie decided to transfer fuel from five-gallon cans stored on deck to the main tank. David tried to talk him out of it, saying that one wave would have the deck awash and seawater in the fuel tank. Leslie insisted that it was calm enough, so David reluctantly prepared to help him. On deck, Leslie changed his mind, saying that it had suddenly become rough. It was Leslie's frustration at work: He felt compelled to take some action, and the fuel transfer was the first thing that came to mind.

Over the four days and nights of the gale, *Aqua Star*'s teak bowsprit cracked under the pounding, and she was thrown 111 nautical miles off course. Finally, on August 30, David reported that *Aqua Star* could make four knots on course in more manageable seas:

> We are all somewhat disheartened and cannot be optimistic, but rather we wait for weather to close down on us again. Still, we are moving toward the rig.
>
> 6 P.M. We are still making four knots on course of 280°— right on rig. Now only 14 nautical miles away. Now we speak positively but still dispassionately of maybe seeing it by morning after a night of heaving-to.
>
> 7:30 P.M. I'm on the helm. Gay pokes her head out of the companionway to puff a cigarette. She says, "Maybe later we will be able to pick it up on the radar. I'm dying to see it."
>
> I said, "Well, come and take a look; there it is." Everyone

In the middle of Hudson Bay, Neddrill II, *drilling for* Aqua Star's *sponsor, Canterra Energy, watched the yacht's progress through the storm.*

The journey almost complete, Neddrill*'s kitchen produced a cake for* Aqua Star*'s crew.*

tumbles from below and we laugh and yell. This is really a big moment. We contact them on the radio. They see us. "You are 9.2 nautical miles away." A little over two hours. It will be too dark to film.

We transfer to *Neddrill II.* The way we transfer sticks in our minds. A small motorboat draws up alongside *Aqua Star.* Our gear is tossed to the men aboard, who stow it. [David lost more points in the women's books for having to be reminded to take a camera aboard the rig.] Now it's our turn and there is no way to leap gracefully, as both *Aqua Star* and the launch heave and bob independently; the space between them one moment is inches and the next yards. It's a wet ride to the *Arctic Schiko,* an icebreaker/supply ship. A rope ladder is dropped over its side. Carolann lifts her foot to step on the bottom rung, but in an instant the *Arctic Schiko* lifts on a wave and the bottom rung is out of reach over her head. Eventually we are aboard, laughing. The powerful engines of the *Arctic Schiko* quickly bring us along-side *Neddrill II.* A crane lowers what looks like a three-meter-high bird cage made of rope, with a rubber-disk floor. Our ditty bags are tossed onto the floor. We stand on its outside edge, grasping the rope cage, and are lifted aloft and swung over onto the *Neddrill II* and deposited in a heap on deck.

Instantly, a man named Ken greets us, whisks us to our cabins. We shower, put on clean clothes, and feel human again. Our laundry is left in bags outside our cabin doors. We meet at Ken's room and are made to feel at ease. There is no drinking allowed on *Neddrill II*. After a delicious supper (for some reason, we all drank glass after glass of foamy, cold, rich milk) with desserts of pies, ice cream, cakes, etc., we lean back in our chairs to answer questions from crew members in the spacious dining area. We bounce off walls as we visit the bridge. Leslie and I soon pile into our bunks, but the girls watch videos till 4 A.M. Our clothes, neatly folded, are hanging in bags on our doors.

Leslie visited the bridge before turning in. Captain Hoek saw the worried look on his face as he peered out into the darkness for a glimpse of *Aqua Star* being towed around endlessly by one of the supply ships. "Don't worry, Captain, your boat is well looked after," he said.

Neddrill II is fixed over her drill hole by powerful engines. A crew of 90 or so lives aboard her in style while drilling is going on: seamen, engineers, geologists—a wide range of men from all over the world, including Inuit and Europeans. The ship is a marvel: Not surprisingly, the Canterra staff on board frequently quipped, "We *have* the technology." Now the *Aqua Star* crew became tourists, enjoying the ship's hospitality and being fascinated by the scope of her facilities.

Earlier, Gay had sent a message via Polestar indicating that *Aqua Star* was crossing Hudson Bay:

Aqua Star Expedition is in difficulty, but not distress. Have been battling gale-force winds, very high seas, for five days now in middle of Hudson Bay. *Aqua Star* has radio contact with *Neddrill II,* Canterra drilling operation, who offered assistance should *Aqua Star* require it. Food supply okay, fresh water low. *Aqua Star* crew prepared to battle it out, despite snow, hail, fog,

and subzero temperatures to date. ETA Churchill, seven to
10 days.

This was what Gay called "keeping the media interested," and it
was the message I received when I arrived in Churchill on August 29.
I had flown in from Toronto with Matt Phillips, the CITY TV cameraman who figured prominently in Gay's diary. Matt helicoptered
directly to *Neddrill II* from Canterra's base in Churchill—a surprise
for Gay and good material for his own report.

As a yachting writer, I had spent time in Newport, Rhode Island,
waiting for Observer Singlehanded Transatlantic Race sailors to
arrive. Often, those times had been tense vigils. Now I waited in
Churchill for *Aqua Star*—but there really was no comparison. The
drama in Churchill was minimized by the fact that shortly after I
arrived, the crew of *Aqua Star* reached *Neddrill II* and spent 24 hours
aboard enjoying unlimited food, sleep and laundry service before
making a cakewalk of the 175 miles left to Churchill.

In town, I met a man who was waiting to meet Leslie Sike. He was
a northern old-timer with maybe just a touch of hostility toward this
southerner he'd heard about, and he was armed with photographs and
old magazine articles showing boats with sails on Hudson Bay. He
was all set to prove that The First Canadian Sub-Arctic Sailing
Expedition was not the first. I considered explaining to him that the
photographs he showed me were of fishing trawlers and that their sails
were riding sails—for stability and not power. But I thought that perhaps the addition of SatNav, radar, and depthsounders compensated
for the degree of difficulty added by sails, so I just listened to his stories. I'd let Leslie himself defend his right to be first.

The next day *Aqua Star* was once again underway. Around midnight, within view of the lights of Churchill, Leslie dropped the sails
and just drifted around:

> We motorsailed slowly, because we knew we wouldn't be able
> to make port in the daylight, and radioed our ETA for Tuesday
> morning between 10 and 11. Around midnight, I could see the
> lights of Churchill, the grain elevators, and the airport. My crew
> was sleeping. I dropped the sails and just bobbed around. I idled

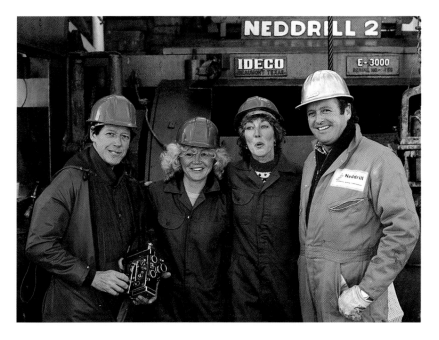

David, Gay and Carolann posed with their guide to Neddrill II's *amazing drilling system.*

the motor to charge the batteries because all the outside lights were on, radar, everything.

Sitting in the cockpit by myself, I silently thanked God for our safe arrival. I thanked my wife for sticking with me; the crew, for they not only had to endure the voyage and weather—they had to put up with me, and that's not easy; then *Aqua Star,* my sweetheart, for she is not only beautiful, but tough, and she proved it. And finally, I forgave Aunt Susie, removing the curse forever.

The next morning, according to David, Leslie began shouting at 6 A.M. that they should have entered Churchill the night before instead of waiting to have pictures taken: The weather had become very windy, with rough seas from offshore. David said that Leslie had motored away from Churchill during the night, and now it was going to be tough pounding getting back. But this was Leslie's finest hour. Here's how he saw it:

With five miles to go, the crew breaks out the champagne.

As if nothing had ever happened during the previous 10 days, this morning we awoke to the most perfect weather in the whole Arctic—beautiful sunshine, 15- to 20-knot winds, just great sailing.

At 10 A.M. we were five miles from the harbor entrance. A helicopter showed up and asked us to sail around a bit for photos. He then told us to drop our sails and just sit and wait for the tugboat *William N. Toulin,* which would be our escort boat into the harbor. There was also another smaller tug, *George Kidd,* escorting us from the rear. Quickly we opened a bottle of champagne and drank a toast to "Us" this time.

Entering the Churchill River, we could see people lining the shores, waving their arms, and car horns could be heard. We tied up alongside the *Takapu.* The crew of *Takapu* lowered a ladder and *Aqua Star*'s crew one by one went up. I followed them, across the deck of *Takapu* and over to the other side. Stepping onto land, I kneeled down and kissed terra firma. It felt good, again I felt that hard lump in my throat, but I held back—too many people, besides . . . big boys don't cry.

Someone handed me a telegram. It was from the icebreaker *Norman McLeod Rogers,* and it read,

"Congratulations and welcome to the Brotherhood of Arctic Sailors."

Signed: Captain Gerard Guesneau

And so it happened. A goal was reached and a dream fulfilled.

Aqua Star was the first sailing yacht ever to cross Hudson Bay and enter the Port of Churchill in Manitoba.

After 108 days and 3,600 miles, the expedition was a success!

Aboard the *William N. Toulin,* there were snickers when Leslie asked the pilot to be sure to take a deep passage, because *Aqua Star* drew eight feet. "Where does this guy think he is?" and "Who does he think he's talking to?" were the questions they asked as they led *Aqua Star* into the port. The *William N. Toulin*'s usual job is leading 700-foot grain freighters in and out of the harbor. In spite of the guidance of these Churchill experts, Leslie was still nervous, and still second-guessing, trusting no one but himself.

There had been some controversy aboard *Aqua Star* about whether David should be transferred to the pilot boat to photograph *Aqua Star*'s triumphant entry to Churchill. But David wanted to complete the voyage on *Aqua Star,* so he stayed on board until they had entered Churchill and then photographed *Aqua Star* being rafted up to the Canterra supply ship, *Takapu.*

Aqua Star was greeted by a clutch of townspeople, some Canterra staff members, the mayor of Churchill, and a few people who consti-

Captain Leslie Sike

tuted the media: me, Matt Phillips, and Peter Earle (from the steel company Dofasco—a sponsor David had recruited). No one really knew why they had done it, but everyone there accorded the crew the respect that comes from achievement. Leslie was in the limelight for a few hours, while the rest of the crew, clearly happy to be there, looked around them, wondering where to begin picking up the threads of their everyday lives.

Gay made tracks: She was getting as far away from *Aqua Star* as possible and was barely speaking to any of the others. David was still his quiet self, smiling and relieved to have completed the job. But Carolann was tired and tense, clearly distraught, and not able to see what the future held. Not once in his account of the trip did Leslie mention the feelings and tensions on board. That was just his way, as he had told Gay: If he hadn't actually thrown anyone overboard, they were okay. He thanked them in his thoughts, in his diary—but he remembered Captain Guesneau's message as though it had been sent to him alone: Welcome to the brotherhood of Arctic sailors. Carolann also recorded the text of that message:

> To: Captain Leslie Sike and the Crew of *Aqua Star*. Congratulations on the wonderful voyage you have just com-

Carolann Sike

pleted. All of us on board are proud of you for this successful achievement. You are now part of the Canadian Arctic brotherhood. Carolann, Gay, David, and Leslie, bravo de nous tous du *Rogers.*

You deserve a good rest before returning back to Toronto and I hope your return journey next year will be as successful. The crew of this vessel and I are looking forward to see you in the Arctic next year.

Chapter Twelve

❦

Churchill, Manitoba

Sailing into Hudson Bay is only a little like climbing Mount Everest. The bay is most certainly, overwhelmingly, *there,* but it is hard to imagine the rewards due to its conquerors centuries after it was discovered, claimed, and explored. No view from a great height; no knighthoods; no real fame. Only a small notoriety, a wealth of experience, and the nationalistic pride of seeing Canada's real wilderness and meeting its people. That's what the crew of *Aqua Star* took home with them from Churchill.

In some ways, Leslie Sike's expedition belongs to the extremes of the sailing world—but he did, after all, often meet and talk to fellow yachtsmen who had sailed the Labrador Coast. For the crew of *Moby Dick,* it was a summer vacation cruise.

In 1986, the Cruising Club of America informed a very disappointed Thomas Watson, Jr. (former head of IBM, and then United States ambassador to the Soviet Union) that a Canadian yacht had successfully crossed Hudson Bay in 1985, foiling his plan to be the first. So Leslie had had good reason to keep a watchful eye out for competition. And he had good reason to feel that he had accomplished something significant when the voyage was complete. He did make the record books, and he did set himself apart "from the other five billion people out there."

Like his heroes the Smeetons, he had sampled the thrill of passagemaking. On his first voyage as the captain of a vessel, Leslie Sike, Gay's "Captain Vicious," was the catalyst, the leader, the rock of Gibraltar when the going got rough—the hardest person in the world to please and the one person to whom everyone on board wanted to prove themselves. In a way, my boss had been right: There was a degree of maniacal control exerted by Leslie on his crew. But they were volunteers, and they had in common the desire to go down in the record books. I believe, however, that experience is not lost on Leslie, and that he learns from his mistakes—he may not always be the scourge of feminism that the diaries depict.

For anyone who has ever shared quarters below decks on a cruise, the tensions aboard *Aqua Star* will come as no surprise. Considering that the crew comprised four people with four different motives and goals—some of which were in conflict—it's surprising that things were not worse. Certainly their respect for one another returned even as they disembarked at Churchill. Each one of them praised the others for their contributions; each one expressed the thought that the four of them, as a team, had succeeded, and that they were proud of one another. Even in their diaries, stress-releasing malicious scrawls are interspersed with praise or gratitude for this action or that quality someone else had displayed.

Leslie, for all his volatility, never led them into danger and always took decisions quickly and firmly. He never vacillated, and, once having shouldered the burdens of the captain's role, never let them down. He assumed the privileges of the rank from the outset too, but that should have surprised no one.

Carolann never wavered in her efforts to make Leslie's vision a reality. And she made sacrifices for that vision, often with little regard for her own best interests. The voyage taught her a great deal both about making that kind of sacrifice and about the dynamics of her marriage. Although it seems like hard-won knowledge, that is wisdom, I think.

Although Gay's record for the expedition seems full of incident, accident, and invective, her steady, competent work aboard *Aqua Star* made a great deal of difference to its success. In Churchill, she proudly displayed her well-defined biceps and crowed about her ability to lift the anchor with the problematic 40-pound lead pig that Leslie used to weight the anchor chain. And no one should ever underestimate the discipline it takes to prepare meals on schedule, day in and day out, for hungry sailors with demanding tastes. Discipline may have been a stumbling block for Gay in port, but underway she did herself credit.

And as for David, the enigma, his film may be incomplete due to lack of funds for production, but his diary provides the most complete record of The First Canadian Sub-Arctic Sailing Expedition. He went along for the ride and proved to be a careful observer—good at listening and more interested in learning about others than in expressing himself. As the oldest member of the crew and the least experienced, he was often tired, bruised, and sore. But, always tight-

Hauled out in Churchill Harbor: Aqua Star *wouldn't cross Hudson Bay again.*

David Farr, Carolann and Leslie Sike and Gay Currie: the voyage complete.

lipped, he kept it to himself, he noted later in his diary, so they wouldn't think he couldn't do his job.

So they all four deserve the glory reserved for those who follow "great matters" to their completion.

From Churchill, Leslie and Carolann accepted Canterra's offer of a lift to St. John's, Newfoundland, with *Aqua Star* welded to the deck of a supply ship. Both were only too happy never to cross Hudson Bay under sail again. "That bay is unreasonable," Leslie said. "The water doesn't have waves, it boils. I don't want to go through it again."

In St. John's for the winter, the Sikes put their lives back in order, and after a few months, Carolann began to climb out of the depression the expedition had wrought. It seemed that without the pressures of the expedition, the relationship between the two of them came back into focus and, not without pain and setbacks, they recovered their equilibrium. They were both wiser, and Carolann felt that she had learned how to protect herself from the worst of the perils of life with Leslie.

In the summer of 1986, Leslie and Carolann took *Aqua Star* back up the seaway to Toronto and began to plan their next adventure. In August 1990, *Aqua Star* sailed into the port of Leningrad. "To Russia with Love," the Sikes called their second expedition, becoming the first Canadian yacht to enter St. Petersburg (as Leningrad was shortly renamed).

Back in Toronto, Gay Currie carried on exploring, this time for a career that made sense for someone with her wanderlust. Looking back on The First Canadian Sub-Arctic Sailing Expedition, she considered that it was all high adventure—and she wanted more of it.

David Farr chose for his next expedition a passage along the Labrador Coast to revisit the communities where he had sat in local clinics to write in his diary, where he had basked in hospitality and been amazed by the fact that the people he met cared enough about their well-being to offer *Aqua Star*'s crew their homes and other comforts. David fitted out a trawler and loaded it with children's toys and clothes to give away, expecting to spend a summer season on the coast, but he was forced to stop in Quebec City when his vessel had engine and other problems.

Looking back, they all say they wouldn't have missed it. They are proud of their adventure, grateful to the boat that Leslie built for her strength and security, and pleased, above all, to have had the experience. Yes, they say, it was something well worth doing.

EPILOGUE

※

THE VIEW FROM SHORE:
TEN YEARS LATER

On our trip, I had observed the poverty of many of the Inuit. With the help of individuals, schools and churches, I gathered three tons of children's clothing and packed them aboard my 42 foot, 40 ton 1934 steel tugboat and started down the St. Lawrence River. Unfortunately, I had a bout with cancer so the clothes went north without me.

Since then, *Arctic Blue* has sailed the Great Lakes, and I hope to spend more time on the St. Lawrence River and Lake Superior, especially when my wife retires from her teaching job. This winter, a friend from Oregon has invited me to sail "to Mexico and beyond, until it gets too hot."

For anyone contemplating cruising with others, I would like to caution them: be prepared for the inevitable squabbles, hurt feelings, and harbored grudges. These challenges will be offset through the bonding that develops when people share serious experiences.

There were dangerous life-threatening times when we were aboard *Aqua Star,* and times when we silently drank in the absolute beauty of the moment. And there were fun times, too, when we rocked with laughter. This trip changed my life. I became more aware of what is really important in life. It became easier to say, "It doesn't matter."

Leslie, Carolann and I keep in touch and visit back and forth. I love them dearly and feel blessed to have such fine people as good friends.

DAVID FARR, *November 1994*

⚜

To sail the sub-Arctic had been Leslie's and my dream for 10 years. Once we had committed ourselves to it there was no turning back. This was the real test . . . not to give up, no matter what. Our ultimate reward was to ourselves . . . that we had been successful and had accomplished our goal. We experienced a high that only a few people in a lifetime would ever know . . . a feeling that cannot be expressed appropriately with words.

Leslie was the catalyst. He was tough, (but tougher on himself than anyone else) so that his feelings would not get in the way of his making the right decisions. I believed that David, after making the trips down the St. Lawrence River in his own boat *Arctic Blue* the following season, en route to the Labrador, can now fully appreciate why Leslie trusted only himself.

As a team we started out . . . each one of us, Gay, David, Leslie and I, fulfilling our own specific roles on board during those 108 days . . . and as a team we were successful. Speaking with David and Gay many months later after the expedition was behind us, we all agreed, the ultimate experience of our lives had been sailing to Hudson Bay. It has provided us with memories to cherish for a lifetime (good and bad; with highs and lows . . . the whole gamut of emotions). We have a special bond linking us together because of this experience and will remain friends forever.

The following year, Leslie was presented with the 1986 Cruising World Medal for Outstanding Seamanship. We also received an award from the Newfoundland Cruising Club, letters of recognition from the mayor of Toronto and the prime minister of Canada, and many other citations from clubs and organizations.

The people who befriended us en route from Toronto, Newfoundland, Labrador and Manitoba, will never know just how much we appreciated them and how touched we were by their moral support of our dream, their generosity in providing baths, laundry facilities, food, and other comforts. We will never forget their companionship. Forever each one will have a very special place in our hearts.

Leslie and I set out once again in 1989 and were successful in completing another expedition, to be the first Canadian sailing yacht to enter the port of Leningrad (since changed to St. Petersburg) on August 3, 1990. After 3½ years, *Aqua Star* arrived back home in Toronto, in September 1992.

We are giving slide presentations of both our expeditions to yacht clubs, Power & Sail Squadrons, corporations and other interested groups. After 10 years of living aboard, it is somewhat disturbing to not feel the lap of water on *Aqua Star*'s hull, and so we are once again stocking up on "freedom chips" to sail *Aqua Star* to places she has never been before. As Leslie would say, "It's all right to dream, but get after it. They don't just happen, you have to make them happen."

Leslie and I recently celebrated our 25th wedding anniversary. I can only say, that if the next 25 years are as exciting and rewarding as the last, then . . . it was all worth doing.

CAROLANN SIKE, *November 1994*

APPENDIX

✿

AQUA STAR *FACTS*

Custom-built, Ted Brewer-designed cruiser, cutter rig, soft-chine
   welded-steel construction
Builder: Huromic Metal Industries, Leslie Sike
LOA: 50 feet
LOD: 41 feet
DWL: 32 feet
Beam: 12 feet 9 inches
Draft: 7 feet
Displacement: 27,000 pounds
Ballast: 8,400 pounds
Engine: 61 hp
Sail area: 900 square feet
Fuel: 162 Imperial gallons
Water: 70 Imperial gallons
Hull speed: 7 knots
Fully commissioned weight: 20 tons

AQUA STAR'S EQUIPMENT, PERSONAL SAFETY & CLOTHING INVENTORY

Raudaschl sails—seven bags (9⅜ oz. Dacron triple-stitched)
Brookes & Gatehouse speed log
Brookes & Gatehouse depthsounder
Sailor VHF radio
Raytheon 1200 radar
Wagner hydraulic steering
Wagner S50 autopilot (never connected)
Motorola SSB radio
Walker 402 SatNav
Omega Tracker Navigator
Wagner seven-inch magnetic compass, externally gimbaled
Cestral Major six-inch magnetic compass
Volvo Penta four-cylinder 61 hp diesel
Racor fuel filter and water separators
Antarctic diesel cabin heater
Schatz barometer 2 in millibars, inches and centimeters
Schatz ship's clock, eight-bell
Seth Thomas quartz chronometer (2)
VDO engine-hour meter
Kerosene two-burner cooking stove with oven
Three Guest 630 EPIRBs
Four personal xenon strobe lights (Guest)
One Guest man-overboard xenon strobe light with life ring
Two 300,000 cp hand-held Guest searchlights
Zodiac 12-foot dinghy with 9.9 hp Evinrude motor
One 25-man life raft (the smallest Canterra owned)
Four Narwhal immersion suits (offshore oil rig survival suits)
One Honda 600W generator
Mada marine oxygen unit
161 charts; various sailing directions, tide charts, magnetic varia-
    tion charts
Ebco plastic sextant
Extensive medical and first-aid supplies; vitamins and Transderm
    5 (for seasickness)

One 12-gauge shotgun, one 30-06 rifle, one 303 rifle and
  ammunition
45-Imperial-gallon kerosene tank
Spares for engine, electrical, mechanical, rigging; repair materials
  and tools—approximately 2,000 pounds total
Ground tackle: one 45-pound plow anchor, one 45-pound Bruce
  anchor, one 30-pound Bruce anchor, one 260-foot ⅜-inch gal-
  vanized chain, one 175-foot ⅜-inch galvanized chain, 3,200
  feet assorted lengths and diameters of braided GWB nylon
  anchor rode
S&L 555 manual double-action two-speed lever windlass
Two Bolex 16 mm movie cameras, plus assorted lenses
Six Canon still cameras, plus lenses
20,000 feet of Kodak 16 mm color movie film
100 boxes of 36-frame Kodachrome film
Four tape recorders
Flotation coveralls
Safety harness
Lifejackets
Foul weather gear & boots with felt liners
Thermal underwear
Wool socks, sweaters & gloves
Leather mitts
Scarves, hats & balaclavas
Goggles
Vuarnet Nautilux Sunglasses
Tilly Endurable, Inc. clothing
Sebago moccasins and Sailing Boots
Trekk Subarctic Sleeping Bags

LIST OF SPONSORS

CANTERRA ENERGY

MRS. M. ALDIS

AQUA SIGNAL

BGR MACHINING CO. LTD

BOOTS DRUG STORES
(CANADA) LTD.

CIBA-GEIGY CANADA LTD.

DURACELL INC.

EXCELL WIRE EROSION
(CANADA) LTD.

MR. & MRS. G. FECTEAU
Willowdale, Ontario

G. & B. PENNEL

GUARANTEE FIT INC. (TREKK)

GENERAL FOODS INC.

G.W.B. ROPE & TWINE INC.

HARBOURFRONT,
York Quay Centre

INTERNATIONAL PAINTS
(CANADA) LTD.

KODAK CANADA INC.

LABATT'S

CHATEAU-GAI WINES

LEMANIA COMPANY

MADA MARINE OXYGEN INC.

MAGIC PANTRY FOODS INC.

MASON'S CHANDLERY
'THE STORE'

MELITTA CANADA INC.

MERIDIAN MARINE INC.

MESZAROS ELECTRIC CO. LTD.

MINISTRY OF FISHERIES
AND OCEANS, CANADA

NABISCO BRANDS LTD.

MRS. E. NADIN

RACOR INDUSTRIES, INC.

RAYMOND LANCTOT
(1982) LTEE

RAUDASCHL SAILS

SEBAGO, INC.

SHOPPERS DRUG MART

MRS. R. SINCLAIR

MR. & MRS. K. STAUFFER

MR. P. SUTHERLAND

THE GUEST CORPORATION

THIRD QUARTER COMPUTING

TILLEY ENDURABLES INC.

TOM TAYLOR CO. LTD.

TORONTO HILTON
HARBOUR CASTLE

TREBLEX LTD.

MR. D. TRUMBO

VUARNET FRANCE

WAGNER ENGINEERING LTD.

WOOLCO DEPARTMENT STORES